Prophet from Plains

Prophet from Plains

Jimmy Carter and His Legacy

FRYE GAILLARD

Foreword by David C. Carter

The University of Georgia Press ATHENS & LONDON

© 2007 by the University of Georgia Press
Athens, Georgia 30602
All rights reserved
Set in 10.5 on 14 Monotype Garamond by Bookcomp, Inc.
Printed and bound by Thomson-Shore

The paper in this book meets the guidelines for permanence
and durability of the Committee on Production Guidelines
for Book Longevity of the Council on Library Resources.

Printed in the United States of America
11 10 09 08 07 C 5 4 3 2 1

Library of Congress Cataloging-in-Publication Data

Gaillard, Frye, 1946–
Prophet from Plains : Jimmy Carter and his legacy /
Frye Gaillard ; foreword by David C. Carter.
 p. cm.
Includes bibliographical references and index.
ISBN-13: 978-0-8203-2914-7 (hardcover : alk. paper)
ISBN-10: 0-8203-2914-2 (hardcover : alk. paper)
1. Carter, Jimmy, 1924–
2. Carter, Jimmy, 1924– —Political and social views.
3. Carter, Jimmy, 1924– —Influence.
4. United States—Politics and government—1977–1981.
5. United States—Foreign relations—1977 –1981.
6. Presidents—United States—Biography.
7. Ex-Presidents—United States—Biography. I. Title.
E873.2.G35 2007
973.926092—dc22 2007006691

British Library Cataloging-in-Publication Data available

To the memory of David Halberstam,
the best and the brightest,
and of Marshall Frady,
who transformed journalism into an art

The prophet is a man who feels fiercely.
God has thrust a burden upon his soul,
and he is bowed and stunned
at man's fierce greed.

Rabbi Abraham Heschel

Contents

Foreword

Not long after Jimmy Carter left the White House, Frye Gaillard became one of the first American journalists to write a serious retrospective on his presidency. Gaillard's groundbreaking series in the *Charlotte Observer*, published in the summer of 1985, drew praise from a wide variety of sources. Jack Nelson, Washington bureau chief for the *Los Angeles Times*, called it "a great contribution to the literature of the presidency." The songwriter and novelist Tom T. Hall, a close Carter friend, called it "near genius." And James Wall, editor of the *Christian Century* magazine, in a letter to Gaillard, summarized the series this way: "You certainly had to note the failures, and I think you are on target with the reasons for the failures. But you have done something few other journalists have done. You have identified Carter's strengths and have properly put his religious faith at the center of his being. . . . I trust that this will be a first step toward restoring Carter to his proper place in world history."

Wall's comments proved remarkably prescient; Gaillard's retrospective became one of the earliest and most important reassessments of Jimmy Carter's tenure in the Oval Office, a bellwether of subsequent scholarship on the thirty-ninth president and his legacy. Not insignificantly, Gaillard was also one of the first to

sense the dynamic possibilities of Carter as an actor on the national and global stage following Ronald Reagan's 1981 inaugural, as a presence who was not content to "go gently into that good night" of relative obscurity. It is thus fitting that two decades after his initial retrospective, Gaillard has returned to the subject of Jimmy Carter, significantly expanding his initial writings to illuminate the Georgian's quite remarkable postpresidency, unrivaled in the annals of modern presidential history. In addition to Carter's much publicized work with Habitat for Humanity, Gaillard writes about his efforts through the Carter Center, a nonprofit organization based in Atlanta, to combat the ravages of third-world disease, monitor elections in more than two dozen countries where democracy is still both fragile and new, and energetically pursue peaceful solutions to conflicts in many of the hottest trouble spots in the world. As Gaillard so capably demonstrates, Carter has been remarkably consistent in his attentions, and such constancy of purpose has borne some truly impressive dividends.

The portrait of Carter that emerges from the pages that follow is not that of an elder statesman playing it safe but rather a man of rocklike resolve who speaks his mind and accepts controversy as the cost of doing business. As Carter himself has insisted, quoting a childhood teacher, "We must adjust to changing times and still hold to unchanging principles." Roger Wilkins, award-winning journalist, veteran civil rights activist, and official in Lyndon B. Johnson's administration, was asked in 2002 whether Jimmy Carter as an activist ex-president might ruffle the feathers of his successors in the Oval Office. "The answer has to be yes," Wilkins answered emphatically, "because he's a truth-teller. . . . The art of politics is the art of the possible. The art of idealists is showing how things might be." Fundamentally an idealist, Carter has amassed his share of critics through the years who dismiss him as naive—and sometimes as excessively self-righteous and stubborn—and

there have unquestionably been moments when more-recent presidents have perceived him to be more irritant than ally. Gaillard lets the critics have their say and offers his own understanding of Carter's shortcomings. But he writes with authority about Carter's accomplishments. Anyone who reads this book will, at the least, have to take Carter seriously and be reminded of a time not far in the past when integrity and decency were the hallmarks of the presidential character.

During his tenure in the White House in a troubled era in American history, Carter preached the virtues of energy conservation, couching that call firmly in the language of morality. The imperative of careful stewardship over nonrenewable resources and Carter's ongoing attention to a growing environmental crisis seem especially relevant at a time when political satirists write only half-jokingly of an administration flirting with "petrotheism" and a sitting vice president dismisses conservation as little more than "a sign of personal virtue . . . not a sufficient basis for a sound, comprehensive energy policy." In a 1979 speech that has been nearly relentlessly pilloried by critics in the decades since, Carter spoke candidly about a "crisis of the American spirit." We would do well to ponder whether a president's call for national introspection is worthy of such derision and whether our historical verdict of Carter as being held hostage by the awesome weight of presidential decision-making was rendered too hastily. A more judicious appreciation of the intricate calculus of unintended consequences ensuing from America's actions abroad would be welcome in these troubled times when platitudes of progress evoke nothing so much as the Vietnam-era assurance of "light at the end of the tunnel."

In an era where sweeping White House promises made in the klieg lights of meticulously constructed photo opportunities are all too often left unfulfilled after the blinding glare of the media fades, the year-in, year-out nature of Carter's work as peacemaker,

champion of democracy and human rights, and public-health advocate—and the relentless focus on measurable outcomes rather than sloganeering and media spin—offers a stirring counterpoint to the politics of business as usual. Jimmy Carter's example offers a rhetoric of compassion matched by results.

In delivering his Nobel Peace Prize lecture in December 2002, Carter made perfectly clear his belief that in an era of nuclear proliferation absent the constraining bipolar framework of the cold war, "for powerful countries to adopt a principle of preventive war may well set an example that can have catastrophic consequences." His words were not lightly chosen; three months later the United States led a "coalition of the willing" in Operation Iraqi Freedom in what the White House both at the time and in the aftermath has vigorously defended as a policy of preemption or "anticipatory defense." Now more than four years later, the Middle East is a region engulfed in a new and devastating cycle of violence over a widening geography, even when measured against its tragic history of seemingly perennial bloodshed.

Freed from the awesome burden of decisions about national defense and the use of military force that he shouldered as president, Carter as an ex-president has unapologetically given witness to his vision of Christianity as a religion worthy of "the Prince of Peace." More than any other world leader before or since, Carter has helped to enshrine respect for human rights as a national and international value rather than a negotiable expedient, and his commitment to the peaceful resolution of global conflict is similarly unshakeable. John F. Kennedy in the crucible year of 1963 noted, "We all inhabit this small planet. We all breathe the same air. We all cherish our children's future, and we are all mortal." Carter's rhetoric and activism have echoed that lyrical admonition, and in many ways he represents a "voice in the wilderness" in an era when leaders and followers on the various sides of a polar-

ized international arena ironically share a common vision of "evil-doers" arrayed against the righteous. Even with what some have criticized as his inflexibility in dealing with geopolitical realities and national sensitivities, Jimmy Carter has still shown over the decades an appreciation for the subtleties of international diplomacy. Such knowledge is markedly absent from the current dichotomous insistence that "you're either with us or against us." Carter has no patience for such a Manichaean division of the world community.

In the wrong hands, and when wielded too bluntly, historical hindsight can be a clumsy tool. But it can also yield powerful insights; some of the same African American activists who strenuously criticized Lyndon Johnson during his presidency, particularly during its latter stages, were far more sympathetic in retrospect. Julian Bond, for example, lavished praise on the ex-president at the opening of the Johnson civil rights papers in 1972 and explicitly cast aspersions on Johnson's successor, Richard Nixon. "When the forces demanded and the mood permitted," Bond eloquently stated, "for once an activist, human-hearted man had his hands on the levers of power and a vision beyond the next election. He was there when we and the Nation needed him, and, oh my God, do I wish he was there now."

One detects a similar kind of yearning in the growing chorus of accolades for the consistency of Carter's vision over the years since he left office. Although certainly not without his detractors among both knee-jerk pundits and more-measured journalists and historians, Carter has ultimately won the admiration and respect of millions both in the United States and around the globe. Above all else, he is a moving historical target. The mixed judgment of one critic of his White House tenure suggests just how complex a biographical subject Carter remains: "I don't think we ought to put bronze on him yet. . . . He's a wonderful, admirable human being

with great moral values. He was not a successful President. But what he's doing is devoting his life to things that really count. . . . We should celebrate him for that."

We are exceedingly fortunate that it is Frye Gaillard who now offers us a compelling profile of such a fascinating public figure. With the vantage point of a quarter century since Carter left office, it is hard to imagine a more timely moment for such a thoughtful reappraisal. As a fellow southerner, Gaillard, now writer in residence at the University of South Alabama, understands instinctively the regional and religious influences that have shaped Carter's understanding of the world. As a journalist and historian, he brings to his latest subject the same fluid prose and fair-minded clarity that characterized his recently published *Cradle of Freedom*, a majestic and moving narrative of the civil rights movement in Alabama that dramatically broadened the historical cast of characters in that pivotal geography of the African American freedom struggle. As in all his work, Gaillard brings his keen journalistic insights and eye for detail to bear while maintaining the practiced historian's appreciation for larger historical context; not least, his rich appreciation of the southern literary heritage makes for inspiring prose.

When Virginia Durr, a white southerner born at the turn of the century who transcended the clouded vision of time and region to become a lifelong advocate of racial justice, passed away in 1999, she was eulogized by minister and theologian Richard Deibert using the words of the Old Testament prophet Jeremiah: "There is in my heart as it were a burning fire shut up in my bones, and I am weary with holding it in, and I cannot." As Frye Gaillard demonstrates, Jimmy Carter as president, elder statesman, and tireless activist has similarly filled the role of prophetic voice for both the nation and the world. He cannot keep silent, reminding us of our individual and shared responsibility for the least fortunate among us. He has borne witness with his eloquence, but equally

important, has through his hands-on activism offered an example of unflinching engagement and tenacity. We ignore his example at our peril.

David C. Carter
Historian, Auburn University

The Story

The first time I saw Jimmy Carter was on a February night in North Carolina. The weather was terrible—a cold north wind whistling down from the mountains, carrying a mixture of sleet and freezing rain. I wondered what kind of crowd there would be, or if there would be a crowd at all, for this didn't seem like Carter country.

He was speaking that night at Wingate College, the alma mater of Senator Jesse Helms, in the rolling farmlands southeast of Charlotte. I was startled to find, when I made it to the campus, that the Wingate auditorium was filled to overflowing—twenty-five hundred people crowded together in the warmth, cheering Carter's words, laughing at his jokes, asking him questions that were friendly and supportive.

"Mr. President," said one young man near the back of the hall, "I don't have a question, but I'd like to make a statement to you. During the recent presidential election, every time the Carter administration was mentioned, it always had negative overtones. And I'd like to assure you there are people here who were insulted by that. We really believe that due to your integrity, your emphasis on human rights, your struggle with the SALT treaty, that your administration—when viewed from the perspective of history and without biased politics—will be compared favorably with the Truman and Roosevelt administrations."

The crowd responded with sustained applause. Carter simply smiled. "Those are the kinds of questions I like," he said.

This was 1985, barely four years after Carter left office, and he had grown accustomed to such warmth. Outside Washington, where he was still the object of media contempt, the anecdotal evidence was becoming very clear: A grassroots reassessment of Jimmy Carter's presidency—far more favorable than the verdict of the voters in 1980 or the savage judgments of the media for nearly a decade—was already underway, and the reassessments of scholars would follow close behind.

William Leuchtenburg, a University of North Carolina historian and national election-night commentator for CBS, believed the verdict of history was likely to be mixed. But there was little ambivalence, Leuchtenburg noted, when Carter addressed a large and boisterous UNC crowd on a soggy autumn night in 1984. "It was as if he were a rock star," Leuchtenburg said. "The place was filled. There were hundreds of people outside, and when several of us arrived to take seats that had been reserved, people hurled curses at us."

On a national tour in 1985 to promote his newest book, *The Blood of Abraham* (which sold out its first printing of seventy thousand copies in approximately one month), Carter's reception was nothing less than triumphant. From Dallas to New York, the auditoriums were packed. And when he appeared at Central Connecticut University in the town of New Britain, editorial page editor John Zakarian of the *Hartford Courant* was moved to offer this assessment:

> The big story of his appearance was the reception he received . . . several standing ovations and many cheers when he talked about civil rights, disarmament and peace. Most questions from the floor were laced with complimentary remarks.
>
> This wasn't a stacked crowd, carefully selected for its pro-Carter sentiments. It was a cross-section of America. I kept thinking how

many in the audience voted against him. Probably many. . . . With the passage of time comes a change in perspective.

As I began to listen to those kinds of stories, I knew that I wanted to write about Carter, for they took me back to my own first reactions when he burst onto the political scene. As a journalist whose beat was the American South, and as a southerner who had struggled with the sins of our place, I was swept away temporarily by a feeling of promise.

Here was a southerner whose decency and character had been forged in the crucible of civil rights. And with the country reeling from the shame of Watergate and the endless agonies left by the Vietnam War, Carter offered hope for a new kind of pride. He was clearly a man of intelligence, of energy, and of technocratic precision in his thinking. He believed in his abilities and instincts and was totally serious about his ideals. But as time would reveal, he was also a deeply flawed politician.

As president, it seemed, Carter lacked the ability—and maybe even the interest—in selling his policies to the American people, to make them believe and to give them the hope that the problems of the world would not overwhelm us. James David Barber, a presidential historian at Duke University, believed Carter's triumphs, his undeniable accomplishments in the realms of foreign policy and human rights, were triumphs of character. Carter's failings, said Barber, were failings of technique.

Like any summary, that one is probably oversimplified. But it contains its kernel of truth, and it brings into focus the most perplexing question of the Carter presidency: Why didn't it work out a little better than it did? Or to put it another way, how could a man of such integrity and promise—who pursued an ambitious agenda and accomplished much of what he set out to do—find himself, when he ran for reelection, rejected overwhelmingly by the voters?

In 1985, as a writer and editor for the *Charlotte Observer*, I set out

to answer that question in a lengthy series of articles that received a good bit of attention at the time. A decade later, I encountered Carter again when I was writing a book on Habitat for Humanity, the great philanthropic effort, supported by Carter, to build decent housing for the poor.

By then Jimmy Carter's years in the White House only partly defined his legacy. He had been far too ambitious, far too restless and too full of hope, to spend the rest of his life looking back. As much as any other former president, he worked to create a new career for himself, attracting so much attention in the process that some pundits declared, at least half seriously, that he had used the presidency as a stepping stone to greatness.

Certainly, with his work at the Carter Center in Atlanta, he set out to make a difference in the world—to pursue his own vision for peace and human rights that was rooted ultimately in the tenets of his faith. And contrary to the popular understanding at the time, this was not a warm and fuzzy undertaking, the gentle example of an elder statesman taking bows. Carter was far too serious for that, far too stubborn and sure of himself, as he waded into the worst trouble spots in the world, doing what he could. At times he pushed against the boundaries of American foreign policy, much to the annoyance of presidents Ronald Reagan, George Bush (Sr. and Jr.), and Bill Clinton, but in country after country Jimmy Carter helped to stave off wars, eradicate diseases, and lay the foundation for democratic reform.

Historian Douglas Brinkley closed his book on Carter's postpresidency with a couple of lines from the poet Dylan Thomas, which, in Brinkley's view, "perfectly illuminated" Carter's state of mind: "Do not go gentle into that good night / Old age should burn and rave at the close of day."

At the very least, Carter didn't go quietly. Even after winning the Nobel Peace Prize in 2002 and turning eighty a couple of years later, he refused to take his place above the fray. In 2005 he pub-

lished his twentieth book, *Our Endangered Values*, in which he pitted himself against the prevailing political climate of the times. He criticized President George W. Bush, a man he regarded as a national disaster, and spoke out strongly—some would even say harshly—on subjects ranging from preemptive war to capital punishment, some of the most divisive issues of his day.

In the process, he refueled the fury of some his critics. But he also revealed a little more of who he was—a formidable, principled, ambitious public figure, who has left his distinctive mark on the world. At the very least, in these closing years of his life, he has established himself as his country's most powerful voice in the wilderness, a kind of prophet from Plains, standing against the fateful currents of his times.

This book intends to examine his legacy. It is not a presidential biography but rather an extended profile, one writer's understanding of this complicated man, based on encounters off and on for twenty years.

I am grateful for the opportunity to write it.

The Promise

He came from Sumter County, which is like a lot of southern Georgia—a land of row crops and cornfields and brambly pine forests springing from the clay. Andersonville is only a few miles away: an American Dachau, where Union soldiers were held with no shelter during the rainy Georgia winters, where rotten meat was a luxury, and where the bodies—12,912 of them by one official count—were dumped shoulder to shoulder into shallow trench graves, a number pinned to each uniform so that the deaths could be recorded.

The meanness was not confined to the nineteenth century. In 1942 Clarence Jordan, a prominent Baptist preacher with a passion for justice, established—fifteen miles from Jimmy Carter's home—an interracial community called Koinonia Farms. In the county seat of Americus, which would soon gain a national reputation as probably the toughest hamlet east of Alabama, the civic leaders in the Klan and the White Citizens' Council began to pay regular visits to Clarence Jordan's commune.

They came in large groups, usually armed and often hooded. Sometimes they fired their rifles as they drove past in the evening, and on one particular occasion they called Jordan from his house and told him essentially, "You'll be out of Sumter County before the sun goes down."

The preacher, so the story goes, stared back quietly and replied, "I'm mighty proud to meet a man who can control the sun."

Such was the climate in which Jimmy Carter came of age. In broadest terms he shared that legacy with every southern politician of his time. For such men right and wrong were fairly easy to distinguish if they could manage to disengage from the pressures of their place.

From the beginning Carter was more successful at it than most, and in later years the decency he forged in the racial crucible of southern Georgia proved to be at the heart of his political appeal. He was not a crusader in the mold of Clarence Jordan. He was more a real-life Atticus Finch—a prominent and respected citizen of his community who seldom went out of his way to cause a stir. But when events conspired to thrust him into controversy, he didn't duck. When the White Citizens' Council, for example, demanded that he join, pointing out that he was one of the few nonmembers in all of Sumter County and threatening boycotts and other trouble if he didn't, Carter simply refused.

He possessed a kind of bedrock stubbornness, a chilly sense of personal rectitude that would have seemed like arrogance—indeed, his political opponents often regarded it as such—if it hadn't coexisted so easily with humility.

Though the quality was hard to define, it seemed clear enough that he came by it naturally. His father, James Earl Carter—a short and stolid man in the family photographs, dressed in baggy suits, wide at the lapel, cuffs drooping over his shoes—had a reputation as a hard businessman, maybe even a little mean. He and Jimmy never agreed about race. "They got in real arguments," remembers Rosalynn Carter from the early years of her marriage to Jimmy. But James Earl was tough and independent, and the same genes were clearly present in his son. Meanwhile, Jimmy's mother, Lillian Carter, was known for her compassion—and her defiance of convention on the subject of Negroes. She simply never believed

that white people were superior, and young Jimmy, it seemed, had absorbed her inclinations.

All of this became important during the political confusions of the 1970s. In the 1972 presidential campaign the Democrats had nominated George McGovern, and the Republicans had won with Richard Nixon. In the end neither party was happy with its choice. McGovern was too liberal, and Nixon was corrupt, and Jimmy Carter sensed in the moment a perfect opportunity for a man like himself. He would pull the Democrats back toward the center and offer the country a fresh vision of itself: a powerful, honest, and compassionate America, committed to civil rights at home and human rights abroad—a country reconnected to its finest instincts.

His presidential ambitions were fully formed by the time Nixon resigned in 1974. In fact they had begun to take shape before the 1972 election. He had attended that year's Democratic National Convention in Miami with the cadre of young men he would eventually take to Washington—Hamilton Jordan, Jody Powell, Gerry Rafshoon—and they watched as their party went spinning toward the left.

They were not immune to the ideals of George McGovern. Indeed, when the word began to spread that the vice presidential nomination might go to a southerner, Rafshoon and Jordan were quick to push their case. On paper at least, it was less than compelling. Carter had been Georgia's governor for only two years, and although he had enjoyed a brief flurry of national attention by declaring in his inaugural address of 1970, "The time for racial discrimination is over," he was largely unknown outside his native state. McGovern never seriously considered him, and that was probably just as well. Carter was spared the taint of the Democratic disaster, and as he and his aides began to sift through the shambles, the improbable aspiration began to form in their minds. For a time they were reluctant even to confess it to each other. But then,

sometime around September 1972, they decided that the role of supplicant was behind them. As Rafshoon put it at the time, "If we ever come back to another convention, we are not going to wait around trying to have Jimmy chosen."

Soon afterward Rafshoon and Jordan went to Carter and said, "Governor, we'd like to have a talk about your future." They suggested he run for president, and it was a measure of Carter's ambition and his private hubris that two months before the defeat of McGovern—with his party locked in a struggle for its highest ideals—he was, he confessed to his two young aides, already considering a race of his own. Then he smiled and added, "Don't tell anybody, it sounds too ridiculous."

It began to sound less so over the next couple of years, as Nixon's triumph dissolved into scandal and the country began reeling with the shame of Watergate. Though many political observers regarded the idea as lunatic, Carter and many around him believed he could win. There were several reasons for their growing certitude, but primarily that was simply the way Carter was. As Rosalynn Carter has noted, her husband's habit—nurtured by a lifetime of proving the point—was to believe he could accomplish nearly anything he wanted.

He approached every task with boundless energy and technocratic precision. "We memorized all of the state election laws," he boasted much later. "We knew the sequence of events; we knew where our major challenges would be, and I campaigned beginning in January of '75—eighteen months before the election—almost full time."

That Democratic primary season was an impressive achievement for Jimmy Carter. It proved to be a showcase for his greatest political skill: the ability to communicate person-to-person, without the cool and homogenizing intrusion of television. As he traveled around the country, meeting in living rooms and small

convention halls, subjecting himself to the curiosity and skepticism of Democratic leaders, many of them were startled by the force of his intelligence.

"At those kinds of sessions, Jimmy Carter was a genius," said James Fallows, the Washington editor for the *Atlantic Monthly* and a Carter speechwriter before he became disillusioned. "In the primary season, he could see—face-to-face—most of the relevant people. There is, I think, an important contrast between his impressiveness in small groups and his larger difficulties as a political leader. But in 1976, some pretty hard-nosed Democratic leaders—including Averell Harriman and Robert Strauss—came away from initial meetings thinking that Jimmy Carter was FDR."

One of those people was Patricia Derian, a brilliant Mississippian who would later become Carter's assistant secretary of state for human rights. Her venture into politics had begun in the city of Jackson, where, as the wife of a prominent surgeon, she had become involved in the local Head Start Program. In the Mississippi climate of the 1960s any initiative for the benefit of African Americans, even a program to educate little children, was sure to thrust its backers into the realm of controversy. Derian didn't shrink from it, and her house soon became a meeting place for people interested in change. Along with such African American leaders as Aaron Henry of Clarksdale and Mayor Charles Evers of Fayette, she became a stalwart in the Mississippi Freedom Democratic Party, an integrated apparatus that succeeded, in 1968, in replacing Mississippi's segregated regulars as delegates to the national convention.

By the mid-1970s there were a great many people like Patt Derian in the South. They had waged their private battles over the issue of race, first within themselves and later in society. They sensed a new promise for their region of the country, and they were seeking political leaders who shared their aspirations.

Derian remembers an initial skepticism about Carter. But one

morning in the fall of 1975 she talked with him for forty-five minutes in a lounge in the Atlanta airport—just the two of them along with Hamilton Jordan, who had arranged the meeting. Derian was struck by Carter's intelligence, his lack of pretense, and the complexity of his thoughts. But she was also impressed by something more basic: Here was a man whose decency had been steeled by the most important issue of his time, who could project his experiences as a southerner into a sense of mission for America. As Carter would explain it, both at the time and much later:

> I've been a product of an emerging South. I see the clear advantages of our throwing off the millstone of racial prejudice.
>
> I think it's a process that's compatible with the moral and ethical standards of our nation—the heritage of our country, as envisioned by our forefathers. I also see that we have a special responsibility here. When we are meek, or quiescent, or silent on the subject of civil rights at home or human rights abroad, there is no other voice on Earth that can replace the lost voice, the absent voice, of the United States. This is what the persecutors want, and this is what the persecuted fear.

Carter had the ability, said Derian, not only to speak such words extemporaneously but to mean them so obviously that it overwhelmed the cynicism of nearly anyone in the room.

After more than eighteen months of similar performances he managed to tap a surge of southern pride and the national yearnings of post-Watergate America—and with Gerald Ford, another decent man, weakened by his pardon of Richard Nixon and the flagging support of a dispirited party, Carter won a narrow victory. "I tried to be objective," remembered Eleanor Clift, then the White House correspondent for *Newsweek*. "But I was really excited. I thought he was FDR and Harry Truman rolled into one."

Carter was neither, of course, and it didn't take long for the expectations that propelled him, that he had cultivated, in fact, to begin to turn sour. He was a moderate politician whose broad

statements of principle reached most shades of the political spectrum. But when the time came to govern, to make the specific decisions that go along with being president, he was bombarded with disillusionment from the left and the right. The country was still in the aftershock of a national polarization, the bitter divisions of Vietnam, and compromise was not a pretty word.

But his difficulties went beyond the inevitable fluctuations of the national mood or the predictable end of the presidential honeymoon. There were gaps in his abilities as a modern politician. His voice, so steady and sure in private conversation, sounded high pitched and whiny when he spoke to large groups, and his whole persona turned to wood in the presence of a teleprompter.

And there was something even more alarming to Hamilton Jordan, Jody Powell, and the other aides around him: The more exposure he received, the more the American people read and absorbed, the less certain they seemed about who he was. He was a southerner, yes, but he was clearly not a George Wallace. Nor was he a Sam Ervin or Fritz Hollings, those gallantly gray-haired southern politicians given to finespun stories and honey-coated exaggerations of the accent. He was not even a southern liberal in the tradition of Patt Derian. Certainly his instincts ran counter to the thrust of white supremacy—in the 1950s as a school board member in Plains he had worked hard for racial fairness, supporting, among other things, an integrationist plan for consolidating schools. But he made his compromises with the reality of his day; he kept his sympathy private, for example, during the intimidations aimed at Koinonia Farms.

And there was Carter's born-again Baptist faith. He made no secret of it during the 1976 campaign, and although some cynics in the news media regarded his professions as contrived, others understood that he was absolutely serious. But what did it mean? As journalist Robert Sam Anson wondered, after attending a Baptist service in Plains, "What was Carter thinking, sitting there, his

head so deeply bowed, his eyes so tightly shut? What was Jesus whispering?"

The truth, of course, was that Carter seldom listened for celestial whispers. He had read the Bible from end to end on more than one occasion, but there was something unconventional about the way he regarded it: It was not so much a collection of quotes, a catechism for selective application, as it was an account—absolutely relevant—of God's move in history.

"Carter's native intelligence plays out in his faith," maintained Robert Maddox, a former Carter speechwriter and a Baptist minister himself. And along with James Wall, the Georgia-bred editor of the *Christian Century* magazine, Maddox argued that the effect of Carter's religion on the evolution of his presidency was to underpin the finest principles of it—particularly the commitments to human rights and peace. But such connections were difficult for many Americans to understand. Christianity became simply another component of the Jimmy Carter enigma—the fuzzy public picture that seemed, if anything, to lose clarity with time.

"Carter is a complex man," Hamilton Jordan conceded shortly after Carter left office. "And we began to realize, much to our dismay, that even by 1980—after all the millions of words that had been written, and all the thousands of hours on television—the American people still did not have a clear picture of who he was."

None of that might have mattered if Carter had been lucky—if, for example, a navy helicopter and a C130 transport plane hadn't collided in a swirl of Iranian dust, attempting the rescue of fifty-two Americans held hostage in Tehran. But before that disaster and others that occurred at about the same time, there were also the moments that history will have to honor.

The Triumphs

Jacobo Timerman was probably too important to kill outright, so his captors put him in prison for two and a half years and tortured him periodically, according to their whim. But he survived the intimidations of his Argentinean wardens, and if courage and eloquence are the measure of his craft, he established himself as one of the world's finest journalists.

The agony of his country had seen many stages, but arguably the worst began in 1976, when the military seized control of the government and, in trying to combat terrorism, became terrorist itself. Depending on whose estimate one accepts, somewhere between twelve thousand and thirty thousand Argentineans disappeared— spirited away in the night, or sometimes in broad daylight, in sinister Ford Falcons with no license plates.

Timerman's outcry in his newspaper, *La Opinión*, infuriated Ramón Camps, the swaggering police chief in the city of Buenos Aires. But Timerman survived his thirty-month imprisonment, which ended in the autumn of 1979, largely, he claimed, because of the human rights pressures of President Jimmy Carter.

Many Americans regarded that particular Carter policy as naive and semirelevant—perhaps even damaging in the amoral world of international affairs, where the mission of presidents was to pursue a Machiavellian agenda. But in the countries affected by

Carter's human rights obsession, a different view prevailed. The generals were incensed, but the victims took heart; and that was the message Jacobo Timerman wanted to convey on October 9, 1984, when he and Carter finally met at the U.S. embassy in Buenos Aires.

It was an emotional moment. The following spring Timerman remembered the encounter this way:

> We were looking at each other. We are almost the same height, and our faces were at the same level. I said to him, "How do you feel looking at my face, knowing that you saved my life?" His face flushed red, and he looked down and then he touched my shoulder. We Latins, we are used to embracing. But he is an American, a very shy person, and yet you could see that he was moved. He was practically trembling.
>
> There was another man there, a teacher whose name was Alfredo Bravo. He was kidnapped by the authorities at the same time that the Panama Canal treaty was being signed. The American government wanted all Latin American presidents to come to Washington for the signing ceremony. To get the president of Argentina, Gen. [Jorge Rafaél] Videla, to go, there was a promise that no one would discuss human rights. But President Carter, to save one life, broke his word. He demanded that Gen. Videla spare the life of Mr. Bravo.

Much of Carter's human rights policy—the cornerstone in fact—was a simple matter of such persuasion. Sometimes the initiative came directly from the White House—phone calls or personal conversations with the shah of Iran, the military leaders in Latin America, or the various presidents and prime ministers scattered around the world, who viewed it as important to court American good will.

More often, the persuasions were the work of Patricia Derian, the Mississippian whom Carter had named assistant secretary of state, and who, like Carter, found it an easy transition from support

of civil rights in the American South to defense of basic freedoms everywhere in the world.

Derian spent a lot of time traveling. In Indonesia, the Philippines, East Germany, or Argentina, she would gather information from ordinary people: journalists, labor leaders, professors, former prisoners, and especially families of those who had disappeared. Then she would keep her appointments with the waiting heads of state. Typically, she says, the officials began by describing their national constitution—documents that invariably enshrined the highest principles. Then they proceeded to explain the current states of emergency and the need, temporarily, to preserve social order through extraordinary means. Always courteous, but persistently well informed, Derian would reply that the United States desired warm relations but that human rights abuses made this difficult. She tried to be explicit about the details, describing summary executions, torture, or censorship, and would ask what the leaders intended to do about it.

"I tried to deliver my message," remembered Derian,

> which was, "We know everything," and then move things along from absolute denial to admission of reality—which happened in every case. Then they would say, "These terrible things, they happen at the lower level," and you say, "Oh yes, but you are responsible. You hold the title. You are not telling me that you are incompetent?"
>
> It was not a comfortable process. But many of these leaders were intrigued by the conversations, and everybody made some move for the better.

President Suharto of Indonesia released thirty thousand political prisoners, and in Argentina, said Robert Cox, editor of the *Buenos Aires Herald* before attempts to kill his family drove him from the country, "There is absolutely no doubt that Carter policy saved thousands of lives."

Cox, who became editor of the *Charleston News and Courier*, believed Carter soft-pedaled the human rights initiative late in his term. Nevertheless, said Cox, the American policy helped preserve the fragile *idea* of human rights and—along with the economic wreckage over which the military presided—was a factor in the birth of Argentinean democracy.

Many American critics, mostly on the right, denounced the Carter effort as self-destructive and capricious, an inexplicable attempt to undermine our allies. But the vantage point of the world's victims tended to be very different. As Jacobo Timerman proclaimed in 1985, "It was the first time—and I fear the last—in this violent and criminal century that a major power has defended human rights all over the world."

Other Carter accomplishments in the foreign-affairs realm were often as provocative: The American left denounced his increases in defense expenditures; the right was critical of the SALT II treaty on nuclear weapons. A powerful lobby argued against the normalization of relations with China—an accomplishment now widely accepted—and although many conservatives viewed the Panama Canal treaties as a limp-wristed giveaway, other observers understood that those treaties were a step toward stability in Central America.

If such policies were disconcerting to some and difficult to categorize—was he liberal or conservative, cold warrior or dove?—they were nevertheless a reflection of Carter's character and philosophy. He supported human rights because he had no choice. He was a southerner and a Christian, and having read Matthew 25:40 among other verses, he assumed Jesus meant his warning when he declared: "Inasmuch as you have done it unto one of the least of these my brethren, you have done it unto me." Thus, if the United States conspired or acquiesced in the torture of peasants, what did that say about our morality as a nation?

But the application of Carter's values contained other, more

subtle dimensions. He was a student of the late Reinhold Niebuhr, the modern theologian who wrote about the interplay of Christian ethics and the world—the dilemmas of decision that society can compel. Robert Maddox, a Carter speechwriter and fellow Southern Baptist, noted that Carter's critics—particularly those on the left—accused him frequently of moral inconsistency. He opposed torture in Iran, for example, lecturing the shah privately on the evils of the practice. But he also recognized the importance of an ally on the Soviet Union's southern border, and he supported the survival of the shah's regime. "He is a yes-but kind of guy," said Maddox, "comfortable in the presence of competing absolutes."

Maddox remembered one particular briefing for several members of Congress on the SALT II treaty. After Carter offered a detailed explanation of the treaty's contents—a dazzling performance, as Maddox recalled it—the discussion turned to broader questions. One representative asked what Carter would do if he learned the Soviet Union had launched a nuclear attack. Would he really push the button?

"I would not hesitate," Carter replied. The effect was chilling. It was suddenly apparent to everyone in the room that the subject was not, for Carter, an unthinkable abstraction. He had thought about it—coolly and specifically—and although his faith may have whispered, "turn the other cheek," Carter dismissed the notion absolutely as commander in chief. The survival of the world might depend on his resolve, or the Soviet assessment of it, and that understanding had led him to an icy certitude.

On that issue and many others, Maddox was struck by Carter's disdain for the cheap thrill of easy choice, his fascination with the rigor of sorting through his values. And that, at its heart, was the strength of the Carter presidency—his instinctive understanding of morality as a process, an application of values to the world as it is. Carter worked hard at it, and there were those occasional shining moments when it all came together—when his philosophy,

integrity, and boundless supply of sheer energy were brought to bear fully on a challenge that confronted him. The results on those occasions, though admittedly they were rare, went far beyond what many viewed as possible. His pursuit of a Middle East peace, for example, became a kind of monument to the impressive strength of his will.

When Carter arrived at Camp David, Maryland, on September 4, 1978, he knew exactly what the stakes were. "He was convinced," remembered Jody Powell, "that if we didn't aim high and pull it off, the whole Mideast scene could become unraveled. He understood the cost of failure. But he also believed the old diplomatic summary—'significant progress, much remains to be done'—wouldn't fly any more."

Still, Carter's finest hour was his largest gamble. Never in the era of modern hostility had there been a peace agreement between Egypt and Israel. But as Anwar Sadat and Menachem Begin arrived in the foothills of western Maryland, the wash of their helicopters rustling among the birches, Carter knew the setting played to his strengths.

There were no television cameras or large audiences to sway, and the issues, for once, could be addressed in their complexity. It was politics and diplomacy at the micro level, just Carter himself and two other heads of state, flanked by a minimum of aides and advisers. He was convinced that energy and humanity, determination and studiousness, would ultimately prevail—in part, he reasoned, because they ought to.

Both Egypt and Israel had clear interests in settling their dispute—Egypt because Sadat was seeking the return of the Sinai Peninsula, which Israel had occupied since the 1967 war; and Israel because Egypt was its most formidable adversary, without whom the other Arab states couldn't mount an attack.

The problem, of course, was the history of blood hatred and,

not at all incidentally, the incompatible personalities of Begin and Sadat. Carter knew from his earlier hours of study and preparation that Begin was inclined to be a haggler. He was a deeply courageous and patriotic man, willing to risk his life for the sake of his country. But he was also known as a tedious negotiator, stubbornly literal minded and obsessed with minutiae. Sadat was very different. He was bold and moody and even arrogant on occasion, generous and accommodating when it came to detail, but absolutely inflexible on the larger principles that mattered. He liked and admired Jimmy Carter but had little use for Begin even before the negotiations. As Carter would discover, this would only get worse.

The first collision came during the first formal session. Sadat, much to Carter's dismay, had prepared an opening statement that was entirely unreasonable, a militant summary of the Arab position, blaming Israel essentially for every problem in the region. Carter had hoped that Sadat wouldn't read it. For one thing he knew the Egyptian president didn't mean it. Sadat had assured him in advance that he intended to be flexible, but he said it was important for his opening statement to be tough.

As Sadat read his paper, Begin reacted as Carter had feared, becoming visibly agitated at the Egyptian accusations. When Sadat finally finished and the level of tension was on the edge of explosion, Carter, on impulse, responded with humor: "If you'll just sign the statement as written," he said to Begin, "it'll save us all a lot of time."

To Carter's relief Sadat and Begin both laughed, and Begin asked with a smile, "Would you advise me to do so?" But by the next afternoon all amusement was gone, as the clash over issues turned serious and bitter.

The broad outlines of an agreement were easy enough to imagine. Israel would relinquish its political and military control of the Sinai Peninsula, and Egypt would agree to a permanent peace. But

myriad details had to be slogged through, and one sticking point overshadowed all the others: What would happen to Israel's settlements in Sinai? Sadat insisted the settlements were illegal—a point on which the United States agreed—and he demanded unconditionally that they be dismantled. Begin said that was politically impossible.

The impasse was clear by the third afternoon, and Sadat, angry and emotional, rose suddenly to leave. The negotiations had been a failure, he said, and he started for the door. But Carter quickly rose and physically blocked his way: They had traveled too far and the stakes were too high, he said, for the meeting to end so abruptly and on such a note of hostility. He asked for another day to work out a compromise.

Begin agreed, but Sadat only stood there in a silent struggle with his rage. Then after a long hesitation under the demand of Carter's stare, the Egyptian president nodded. One more day turned into ten, and much of the time was spent in confrontation, often bombastic, between Begin and Carter. They clashed about the rights of Palestinians—an issue important to Sadat—and about the settlements in Sinai. On one occasion, remembers Carter, "I stood up for Begin to leave, and accused him of being willing to give up peace with his only formidable enemy, free trade and diplomatic recognition from Egypt, unimpeded access to international waterways, Arab acceptance of an undivided Jerusalem, permanent security for Israel, and the approbation of the world—all this, just to keep a few illegal settlers on Egyptian land."

In addition to the acrimony, however, were creative discussions with Begin's capable aides—chief among them Moshe Dayan, Ezer Weizman, and Aharon Barak—and eventually and incrementally the impasse dissolved. But on the thirteenth day a new dispute arose over an important technicality, and Begin announced again that he wouldn't sign the agreement. The Camp David talks appeared to be dead.

Then came one of those peculiar interventions of luck, a moment that illuminated the humanity of Carter and, perhaps even more so, of Begin. Carter's personal secretary, Susan Clough, arrived at his cabin with some joint photographs of the three heads of state. Begin had asked Carter to sign them for his grandchildren, and Clough, knowing the delicacy of the negotiations, decided to get the actual names so that Carter could personalize the autographs.

Carter did, and despite his discouragement and mounting annoyance at Begin, he decided to deliver the photographs personally. Begin received them on the porch of his cabin, thanked Carter politely, and then looked down and saw the names of the grandchildren. Suddenly he became emotional, repeating each name as he thumbed through the pictures; his lips began to tremble and tears formed in his eyes, and he and Carter talked quietly for a moment, exchanging stories of their grandchildren and making the emotional connection between those stories and peace.

Begin didn't decide right away. But a few minutes after Carter's return to his own cabin, a dejected walk through the woods during which the president reflected on how close they had come, Begin called to announce that he had changed his mind. He would sign the Camp David Accords.

The signing ceremony and the formal treaty that followed in 1979 were probably the greatest triumphs of the Carter administration. Internationally, however, they were only part of a pattern. To much of the world Jimmy Carter offered hope—hope for peace in the Middle East and for simple justice in those ragged countries that were, as the African American leaders once put it in Carter's native South, "sweltering under the heat of oppression."

But there is tragic irony in this observation, for hope is precisely what Carter failed to provide his own country. Instead, Americans got malaise. For the first twenty years after World War II they had lived in the flush of righteousness and power: They had de-

feated an evil empire. But then came Vietnam and a feeling very different, an insidious uncertainty of a kind Americans had seldom known—doubts about both their rectitude and strength. And as newer problems mounted—Iran, inflation, Afghanistan—it became increasingly apparent that Jimmy Carter was not a man who could drive away the feelings.

William Leuchtenburg, the UNC historian, recalled his 1980 election night analysis for CBS this way: "I talked about the sense of things out of control. The producers ended the program with what I was saying as a voiceover across the faces of steelworkers in Youngstown, Ohio. There was just a certain tendency in the Carter administration that had run itself out—the hostages, the economy, a message of limits. There has to be a way to give people hope."

The Fall

On a January day in 1980, Kurt Waldheim found himself sur-
rounded by a screaming mob in the streets of Tehran, and the
UN secretary general—a man accustomed to a certain diplomatic
immunity—thought for a moment that the crowd was going to kill
him. The taunts of the protestors were a jumble—and would have
been even if he had understood Farsi—but then came a sudden,
horrifying gesture that gave a strange clarity to the moment's in-
sanity. They lifted a child, maybe five years old, from the middle of
the crowd. The child had no arms. When he was only three, SAVAK,
the shah of Iran's secret police, had cut them off—a lesson against
subversion within the child's family.

Now, two months into the crisis between the United States and
Iran, Waldheim had come to Tehran seeking the release of the
American hostages—the representatives of a government that had
supported the shah and thus by implication the continuing cruel-
ties of his thirty-seven-year rule.

Waldheim survived his encounter with the mob, those Islamic
radicals who, the previous year, had set out successfully to over-
throw the shah. But even five years later, the diplomat's compo-
sure became briefly frayed as he told the story to Ray Jenkins, a
former staff member at the Carter White House. And the two of
them reflected quietly for a while on the tendency of insanity and

barbarism to produce more of the same—and to engulf even the good people who came within range.

The year 1980 was a terrible one for Jimmy Carter. Day after day no change seemed to come at the U.S. embassy in Iran. Fifty-two American hostages had become the unwilling instruments of their nation's humiliation, and as the months dragged on, the delicate, impassioned negotiations aimed at achieving their release were largely invisible to the American people. The agony began on November 4, 1979, a Sunday morning, when as many as three thousand militants who hated America for its support of the shah poured across the embassy walls and took control of the compound. The Ayatollah Khomeini, the new ruler of Iran, endorsed the attack, and the standoff would last more than a year.

But that was not all. The Soviet Union had invaded Afghanistan, and although Carter's response—a grain embargo, an Olympic boycott, and a backing away from the SALT II treaty—may have represented a forceful diplomatic statement, the Soviets continued with their mission of occupation.

The U.S. economy also was reeling. Oil prices had doubled on the international market, and the shock waves throughout the nation took the form of double-digit inflation, unemployment above seven percent, and investment-paralyzing interest rates. And then there was Senator Edward Kennedy. In 1980 the Massachusetts Democrat decided to challenge Carter for the presidential nomination. Carter promised to "whip his ass" (a quote carefully leaked by the White House staff), and in fact he did so. But Kennedy's challenge became, for Carter, a bitter campaign that left his party divided and confused.

It was as if, said national Democratic leader Robert Strauss, Carter had used up all his luck getting elected in 1976. But the hard truth was that between that election and 1980 Carter had amply set the table for his mounting difficulties.

He had come to Washington as a political outsider—a mantle that he never quite shed and one that he wore with both integrity and self-righteousness. It was an accustomed role, dating back to 1962 and his first run for political office in Sumter County, Georgia—and in retrospect, it is striking to see how thoroughly Carter's approach to the presidency was stamped and circumscribed by his first ventures into politics.

He began in earnest with a race for the Georgia Senate, and he might have won it with little public notice or controversy if a local political boss—Joe Hurst—had not stuffed the ballot box for Carter's opponent. As the *Atlanta Journal* reported at the time and William Greider, then of the *Washington Post*, reported in detail in 1976, Hurst was not at all subtle about it. In full view of anyone who happened to be voting that day, he meticulously cast the ballots of the county's deceased.

Carter was indignant. He filed a lawsuit, which he eventually won, and when the dust had settled and he finally took his seat in the Georgia Senate, his political personality had begun to take shape. As James David Barber writes in his respected book *The Presidential Character*, Carter had settled on an approach to campaigning that included as its first ingredient "a rhetoric of indignation." And Carter's friend and campaign supporter John Pope noticed another transformation: "I saw the real burning desire to win that I had not really seen before. It meant everything to him."

Not that Carter was ever lacking in drive. In his first book, *Why Not The Best?*, he wrote about his time in the navy under the demanding tutelage of Hyman Rickover, an admiral who expected nothing less than perfection. "Why not the best?" was a Rickover notion, and in young Jimmy Carter the words hit to the quick, becoming the underpinning of his resolve.

That quality became more obvious over time, particularly in 1966 when Carter, then forty-two, made his first run for governor. He crisscrossed the state in a little Cessna airplane, often land-

ing late at night in a cornfield in Plains, his mother parked at one end, brother Billy at the other, flashing their brake lights to guide his descent. Carter's principal opponents were the veteran Georgia liberal Ellis Arnall and the eventual winner, Lester Maddox, owner of the Pickrick Restaurant in Atlanta—a man who had made his reputation by shooing blacks from his establishment with an ax handle.

Carter campaigned with his characteristic energy, indignation, and deeply felt appeals to the voters' best instincts. But he came up short, and on election night, when it was clear he had lost, he abruptly left his headquarters and headed back to Plains, so absorbed in his defeat that he forgot to thank Hamilton Jordan and some of his other key workers. Later, after it occurred to him how coldly he had behaved—how much he had been a prisoner of his own self-absorption—he telephoned Jordan to apologize. When Jordan deflected the apology with a compliment about the bravery and determination of Carter's campaign, Carter responded with impatience: "I'm tired of people saying that I ran a good campaign. It wasn't good enough—because I lost. I never intend to lose another election."

So he ran again for governor in 1970, and significantly enough his principle opponent this time was not Lester Maddox but the progressive Carl Sanders, who had served as governor in the early sixties. Carter, once defeated by the right, was now opposed from his left, and after a campaign scarcely less contentious than the first, he won.

Mike Egan saw promise in the victory. Egan, a Republican, was minority leader in the Georgia House of Representatives—a lonely calling in what was then a Democratic state—and he tended to view Jimmy Carter as a fellow outsider. Partly to increase his party's influence and partly because he believed in Carter's plans, Egan largely supported the Carter agenda: reorganization of the state government, environmental protection, some pieces of legislation

to protect the rights of consumers. But Egan was often dismayed at Carter's righteous and confrontational approach to his job. Even much later, after all the years in Georgia politics and four years in Washington as Carter's associate attorney general, Egan still puzzled over the contradictions in Carter's personality.

"He was a totally honest man," said Egan,

> intelligent, hardworking to a fault, and he was fighting the right people to fight. But he wasn't a good legislative politician. He knew a lot more about how to get elected than about how to move things along in the government.
>
> He would just openly do battle with everybody. He got his reorganization through, and some good environmental laws. By and large, he had a credible record as governor. But when he'd lose, he'd always get so mad—the forces of evil were out there—and the lines would firm up.
>
> That's not how you do it. When you have a piece of legislation in Georgia and you want to get it passed, you call some business leaders; talk to them a little—give a little. Don't make speeches and call them names. I felt a little like he did about some of those guys, but Jimmy was just a little too damn sanctimonious about the whole thing.

Speaking in 1985, Egan offered his observations with a smile. At bottom he still admired Jimmy Carter and was proud of his time in the Carter Justice Department, where, among other things, he oversaw the appointment of a record number of women and African Americans to federal judgeships. But Egan understood what Carter never seemed to: that the instincts of an outsider can serve you badly once you've won. As former House Speaker Tip O'Neill would later put it, "When it came to the politics of Washington, D.C., [Carter] never really understood how the system worked. And although this was out of character for Jimmy Carter, he didn't want to learn about it either."

Yet there was another side to the story, for if Carter came to Washington with any mandate at all, it was to depart from business as usual. True, Carter and his aides may have offended the Washington establishment in pointless ways—failing in the early days to return the phone calls of important Democrats or canceling pork barrel water projects without laying sufficient groundwork with the affected members of Congress—but the collision between Carter and established powers was a matter of substance as well as technique. Carter was not a traditional Democratic liberal—a fact that may well have accounted for his election—and he was trying to pull a reluctant party in unfamiliar directions.

He was as liberal as most Democrats on human rights, equal opportunity for minorities, and the pursuit of an arms control agreement with the Soviet Union. But parts of his program were conservative: He was determined to cut the federal deficit (and did—bringing it down from Gerald Ford's $79 billion in 1976 to $27 billion in 1979), and he supported the deregulation of private industry, "orderly" increases in defense spending, and slower growth for social-welfare programs.

Carter was convinced that the combination was precisely what the country was seeking—and certainly his fellow southerner Bill Clinton rode the same understanding in the 1990s all the way from Arkansas to the White House. In the 1970s, it was perhaps understandable that Jimmy Carter was annoyed by the bitter opposition.

Jim Young, a political scientist at the University of Virginia and coordinator of an oral history project on the Carter administration, would argue later that Carter went to Washington with a kind of pristine view of public service. His mission, as he saw it, was to chart the proper course, marshal the strongest arguments, and then the Democrats in Congress—many of whom he had defeated fair and square in the presidential primaries—would fall obediently into line. That didn't happen, of course. The Democratic liberals

believed as firmly in their agenda as Carter did in his, and he found himself trapped between the necessity of compromise and the indignant certainty of his campaign rhetoric.

Soon the press began writing about the "zigzag factor"—Carter's tendency to tack with the political winds. In fact, he was likely no more guilty of that than other national leaders. Certainly, he never reversed himself any more abruptly than President Reagan, who, after a deadly attack on U.S. Marines, retreated from Beirut in 1983, two days after saying he would never do so. But something in Carter's style—and perhaps also in the blurry nature of his image—fed a media perception of irresolution.

And the perception contained its kernel of truth. Carter backed away from his plan to kill thirty federal water projects he regarded as extravagant; by 1978 only a third had been stopped. He pledged to reduce the number of U.S. troops in Korea, then changed his mind. He lectured foreign despots on the subject of human rights, but in many cases continued to aid their regimes. And for nearly two years he postponed a final decision on the neutron bomb. More seriously, in the eyes of many critics, his top foreign-policy advisers were the dovish secretary of state Cyrus Vance and the hawkish national security adviser Zbigniew Brzezinski. Some doubted whether Carter knew his own mind on things as basic as how to deal with the Russians.

In fact, Carter did. William Greider, a political correspondent for *Rolling Stone* and former national editor of the *Washington Post*, conceded that Carter generally had solid reasons for the decisions he made, even those that appeared inconsistent. "Jimmy Carter as a person," said Greider, "is so immensely confident of his virtue and good intentions: that's the anchor he has. But in the presidency, that has no reality at all. People can't see into his heart."

A modern president, maintained Greider, must of necessity translate the complexity of his views and intentions into resonant

symbols—images that communicate in an era of television, where reality is transmitted through short takes and constant changes on the TV screen. "And Jimmy Carter," added Greider, "did not live very well in that world."

In fact, Carter lived terribly in it, and his instincts seemed to get worse all the time. Jody Powell remembered how late in 1979—in the midst of mounting economic problems, with Iran and Afghanistan just around the corner—Carter, a casual jogger whenever he had the time, decided to participate in a six-mile race. He thought it would be fun. But he was not accustomed to running that far, particularly not in the mountainous terrain of western Maryland, and his aides were unanimous in trying to persuade him not to do it.

"We were on the helicopter going somewhere," said Powell, "and I said, 'Mr. President, if you do decide to run that race, which I think is a mistake, just make damn sure you finish.' He just laughed. His attitude was, people drop out of races all the time."

Many years later, Powell still told the story with an air of disbelief, a grimace when he remembered the image that resulted: the president, limp with exhaustion, being helped from the course after approximately four miles. For a beleaguered nation, desperate for reassurance of strength at the top, the picture was devastating.

Carter had a knack for those kind of bungles. In 1980, on the afternoon before his television debate with Reagan, he was struck with what he regarded as a splendid idea: a way to personalize the issue of nuclear war. With some enthusiasm he told his aides of a recent conversation with his daughter, Amy, who had just turned thirteen, in which she had affirmed that the nuclear menace was the greatest problem of the times. The aides, especially Hamilton Jordan and Gerry Rafshoon, tried to explain that it wouldn't work. Most people saw Amy as a little freckled-faced kid, and the conversation, though real, would sound contrived. Carter used it anyway

in the debate that night, and Rafshoon, watching on television, correctly anticipated the derision that would come. He slapped his forehead and groaned, "It's so bad that it's funny."

Perhaps the definitive summary of Carter's clumsiness at mass communication came from Hedley Donovan, former editor in chief of *Time* magazine and author of *From Roosevelt to Reagan*, a widely praised book on the presidency. Donovan thought Reagan was strongest in the area of Carter's greatest failing. With his snappy salutes and winning smile, his flawless actor instincts in the presence of a camera, Reagan had a command of the presidential symbols. He knew how to project both strength and leadership. "And projection," added Donovan, "is part of the real thing."

Yet for all that the country had difficulty making up its mind. Against the backdrop of Iran, Afghanistan, and a failing economy, Reagan tried—understandably—to cast the 1980 election as a referendum on Carter. "Are you better off?" he asked in the TV debate, and some in the Carter camp believe the election was lost at that moment.

But the referendum, it seemed, was more complicated than that. It was as if in the public mind there were two Jimmy Carters. One of them was decent, determined and idealistic, resolutely sane and capable on occasion of boldness and brilliance. His foreign-policy accomplishments were solid, and in the first two-thirds of his term, he had lowered unemployment and the federal deficit, freed U.S. businesses from government restrictions on their ability to compete, and established an energy policy that held promise for the future. Like Ford before him he had largely freed the nation from the stain of corruption, and he embodied a strength of character Americans expected from their leaders.

But if he had satisfied the post-Watergate yearnings for integrity, what about the yearnings after Vietnam—the need for hope, triumph, or even a simple sense of control? Those things seemed beyond Carter's grasp, and the question for many Americans was

whether that was the real Jimmy Carter—a small ineffectual man who was dragging the country down with his presidency.

No doubt there were other issues as well, as the voters weighed their choice: Who was Ronald Reagan? Was he up to the job? Whatever their questions, Americans wrestled with the answers for as long as they could. As late as Monday, November 3, the day before the election, nearly every poll showed a dead-even race.

Then the Ayatollah intervened. Rumors came from Iran that the hostages might be released, and on election eve, all three major networks carried their viewers on a retrospective journey through America's ordeal, which had begun, unfortunately for Carter, one year to the day before the election of 1980.

In his book *Crisis: The Last Year of the Carter Presidency* Hamilton Jordan writes about the call he received in the predawn hours of November 4. It was Pat Caddell, Carter's abrasive young pollster, who had disastrous news from a survey taken immediately after the newscasts: There had been a sudden leap for Reagan, a surge of maybe ten percentage points, and there was simply no way that Carter would recover. "It's the hostage thing," said Caddell. "It's going to be a big Reagan victory."

When the votes were counted, the results were precisely as Caddell had predicted. Once again, the insanity in Iran had become the central nightmare of Jimmy Carter's life—and in the public mind, the definitive metaphor for his failings as a president.

The Final Agony

The hostage crisis was a tragedy for Iran as well as America. In fourteen months it brought down two Iranian heads of state— Mehdi Bazargan and Abol Hassan Bani Sadr—and Iran's foreign minister, Sadegh Ghotbzadeh, found himself on a path of resistance that eventually led to his execution.

But the price Iran paid in political turmoil, kangaroo justice, economic wreckage, and the loss of world esteem was of little consolation in the United States. It was hard, in fact, to see the big picture then, to understand that in the changing face of global politics this was merely a shot across the bow. The cold war terror, imposed on the world by its two superpowers, was about to give way to something every bit as frightening: a surge of Islamic radicalism that propelled not only the Iranian revolution but over the next twenty years would swell into a cry for global holy war that seemed to be heard in every corner of the world.

Again and again the jihadists would strike—in Indonesia and Kenya, in Egypt and Madrid, and at the World Trade Center in New York City. In ironic contrast to that terrible history the hostage crisis of 1980 would eventually seem almost tame, a pale foreshadowing of the terror still to come. But in Jimmy Carter's last year as president, all of that was hard to foresee. Americans, like their president, simply wanted their hostages home and their honor

defended, and when they voted in November, one year to the day after the hostages were taken, their reluctant judgment was that Jimmy Carter had failed.

Perhaps the voters would have reached the same conclusion if the election had been held at a different time. But as the details of the crisis later became clear, they sketched a picture of Carter's character—and his handling of the issue—very different from the one that prevailed in 1980.

Eleanor Clift, the former White House correspondent for *Newsweek*, would later maintain that the ordeal that sealed Carter's political doom may, in fact, have been his finest hour. Others believe that overstates the case. Nevertheless, the final chapter in the fall of Jimmy Carter was the most complex and ironic episode of his presidency.

Whatever limitations or flaws the crisis may have demonstrated, it also revealed a private tenacity that was largely invisible to the American public and a willingness to take risks that contained, by definition, the inevitable possibility of tragedy and failure. The greatest risk and biggest failure came in the form of a rescue mission on April 24, 1980—a portrait of ineptitude that resulted in the deaths of eight U.S. servicemen and ended any chance of an early resolution to the crisis. Jimmy Carter understood the gamble and took responsibility when it didn't payoff. In the years since the mission he found some peace in the knowledge that if he had it to do over, he would make essentially the same decision.

What haunted him at times was another piece of knowledge: that before the mission, in the cloak-and-dagger diplomatic scramble to achieve freedom for the hostages, he and his advisers came very close—a final frustration that only added to a growing string of disappointments.

It was nearly 2:00 a.m., February 17, 1980, when Sadegh Ghotbzadeh arrived. Hamilton Jordan was nervous as he listened to

the footsteps. Diplomacy was not Jordan's field. As Carter's chief political adviser he had organized the brilliant campaign for the presidency in 1976, but now an odd sequence of events had made him a central player in an international crisis. More than three months earlier, on November 4, 1979, a band of young Iranians had overrun the U.S. embassy in Tehran, and fifty-two Americans were still being held hostage. The intractability of the standoff had more to do with internal realities of revolutionary Iran than with the ability of the Americans to push the right buttons, to find the pressure points that would chasten the Ayatollah Khomeini, Iran's impassioned new leader, whose ferocity and radicalism were incomprehensible to Western minds.

There was reason for hope, however. For their own separate reasons both Jordan and Ghotbzadeh, the foreign minister of Iran, wanted to end the impasse, and they had arranged a secret meeting at a plush apartment in Paris.

The meeting was only one component in a vast and tightly orchestrated diplomatic offensive that Carter had initiated in the early days of the crisis. There were intercessions from the Vatican, the UN, even the PLO, as well as from a number of traditional allies and Islamic heads of state. In addition, Carter had suspended all imports of Iranian oil, frozen Iranian assets in American banks, and issued a stern private warning to Khomeini—telling him bluntly that the United States would respond militarily if the hostages were harmed.

All of those efforts, however, had succeeded at most in containing the crisis, in preserving a deadlock that had persisted for months and had begun to test the American people's patience. In the media and elsewhere demands that Carter "do something" grew, and one of the unlucky circumstances of the moment was that most of what he was doing was necessarily secret—contributing to an image of indecision and passivity.

By February 17 Hamilton Jordan was confident the image

wouldn't last. He had traveled to Paris with the highest of hopes—to reconfirm an agreement for the release of the hostages. Like a character in a spy novel in which the plot is too contrived, Jordan, armed with a CIA disguise, had arrived around midnight at the apartment of Hector Villalon, an Argentinean businessman with a taste for high adventure. Two hours later Ghotbzadeh walked in, and despite the strange hour they shared a candlelight dinner of filet mignon.

They briefly matched wits during a round of small talk, and Ghotbzadeh launched into a lecture on the Islamic revolution in Iran. Jordan, however, returned the discussion to the issue at hand. In January, he noted, he and Assistant Secretary of State Harold Saunders had secured an agreement for a resolution of the crisis. They had met repeatedly with two intermediaries, Hector Villalon and Christian Boursruet, a French lawyer on retainer with the Iranian government.

The agreement that resulted involved several steps: First, a five-member UN commission would travel to Tehran and take testimony about Iranian grievances against the United States. The commission would also visit the American hostages, declare their confinement to be inhumane, and supervise a transfer to an official institution, perhaps a hospital. The commission would then issue a report to UN secretary general Kurt Waldheim, and in response Iran would pardon and expel the hostages.

Jordan knew the plan had the backing of Ghotbzadeh, Iranian president Bani Sadr, and the ruling Revolutionary Council in Tehran. He also knew that might not be enough. He was struck by the irony that an agreement that had the support of the entire governmental apparatus of two nations, as well as their elected heads of state, might be countermanded by the Ayatollah, an aging cleric in whose demonology Jimmy Carter had become "the vilest man on Earth."

Already, delays had come in implementing the plan, and Jordan

asked Ghotbzadeh for reassurances that his government could deliver. With a flash of his dark eyes, Ghotbzadeh replied, "Mr. Jordan, you may tell the president of the United States that my government will abide by every detail of the scenario drawn up by you and the French lawyers."

Jordan persisted, however, asking if Khomeini had specifically approved the plan. Ghotbzadeh again seemed affronted and answered that he and other leaders had gone to Qom, the holy city where Khomeini had taken residence, approximately ninety miles from Tehran. They had explained the plan, Ghotbzadeh said, and Khomeini had nodded. "If he had objected to the proposal," the foreign minister concluded, "he would have said so." Hamilton Jordan remembered the jaunty air of certainty.

In the end, however, Khomeini did object. His most deeply rooted instincts were those of a revolutionary, not a traditional head of state. Although Ghotbzadeh and Bani Sadr both saw the devastating effects on Iran—the perpetual atmosphere of crisis that, in their view, impeded the institutionalization of the revolution they had worked for—Khomeini was a man who saw value in the chaos. His ultimate power had resided in the mobs, and he seemed reluctant to alter that climate. Bani Sadr and Ghotbzadeh sought to change his mind, and the debate within Iran prolonged the hostage deadlock through February and March.

By the beginning of April Carter's patience—always far thinner than his public demeanor might have indicated—had expired, and he shifted his attention to something he had considered from the start: a military option.

Before committing himself irrevocably to that course, however, he sent Jordan back to Paris for a final meeting with Ghotbzadeh. This time they began at a more sensible hour, 3:30 p.m. on April 18. Ghotbzadeh seemed tired and fatalistic as he slumped into a chair. "My friend," he said, "I'm afraid it will be a long time before your people come home."

With that, Carter's last remaining doubts were removed, and he proceeded with the most fateful decision of his presidency. On April 24, 1980, eight helicopters left the uss Nimitz in the Arabian Sea, bound for Iran on a rescue mission. Their formidable challenge was to fly across five hundred miles of Iranian desert, under cover of darkness and strict radio silence, to move within striking distance of the embassy. On the way, however, two helicopters developed minor difficulties, and in what critics later regarded as a tragic lapse of judgment, one pilot abandoned his craft in the desert; the other flew back to the Nimitz.

Mission commander Charles Beckwith, an army colonel decorated repeatedly for valor in Vietnam, knew from the start that the rescue was impossible with fewer than six helicopters. He was now down to that minimum. When a third craft developed hydraulic problems after a successful landing at a prearranged refueling station in the desert, Beckwith decided he had to withdraw. Reluctantly, Carter approved the field commander's decision, and then tragedy struck: Still another helicopter pilot, blinded by the darkness and a sudden swirl of dust from the helicopter blades, flew his craft into the side of a c130 refueling plane. The explosion that followed killed eight crewmen.

For a nation searching for images to explain Jimmy Carter, to account, somehow, for the mounting sense of things out of control, the chaos in the desert became a brutal symbol. Even years later it was the way many Americans—and certainly the most cynical and unforgiving members of the news media—interpreted not only Carter's effectiveness as a president but also, it seemed, the very essence of his manhood. He was ineffectual, indecisive, incompetent, timid. As the *Boston Globe* once put it in a startling headline that was published by accident, Carter was a "wimp."

That image was rare, however, if it existed at all, among those who worked with Carter during the Iranian ordeal. Their generalizations were more apt to be these: Carter was an activist president

who, because of his energy and decisiveness, succeeded in containing a dangerous crisis. It did not escalate into a superpower confrontation or a general uprising in the Islamic world. No Americans were executed, and in the end, although it took too long, every hostage came home.

A key ingredient in the survival of the hostages was Carter's early decision on retaliatory force. On November 6, two days after the crisis began and less than a day after it became clear it was supported by Iran's ruling clerics, Carter decided the United States would "blast the hell out of Iran if the hostages were harmed."

On November 23 he refined the sentiment and sent a private message to Khomeini warning that the threatened public trials of the captives would result in the interruption of all Iranian commerce, a step that might mean a naval blockade or the mining of harbors. Any harm to a hostage, Carter warned further, would bring the harshest retaliation. "Khomeini knew I meant it," said Carter looking back. "He never put a hostage on trial. He never injured one."

Gary Sick, a former National Security Council staff member whose 1985 book, *All Fall Down*, was then regarded by critics as the definitive chronicle of the Iranian tragedy, concluded that "Carter's tough private message served its purpose." Sick also believed that, in general, Carter's diplomacy was bold and unconventional and that even the ill-fated rescue attempt was an example, not of indecision or paralysis, but of Carter's willingness to gamble.

Sick's account, however, paints a detailed picture of Carter's largest failing, which occurred long before the hostages were taken. Iran was the place where Carter's values collided: He believed genuinely and deeply in human rights, but the shah of Iran, whose record on the issue was shocking, had been a strategic U.S. ally for thirty-seven years. As time went by, reconciling support for the shah with support for the elemental rights of the Iranian people

became more and more difficult, but Carter gave the dilemma only passing attention. He was preoccupied with other matters, as the American foreign-policy apparatus was stretched to its limits, or beyond, by Carter's simultaneous pursuits of the SALT II treaty, the normalization of relations with China, and a peace agreement between Egypt and Israel.

Iran was a back-burner item until too late, and there was never a systematic reconciliation—or choice—between the competing imperatives of U.S. policy. That had become strikingly apparent on September 8, 1978, when twenty thousand protesters assembled at Jaleh Square in Tehran. The shah's troops ordered them to disperse, and when the crowd refused, the troops opened fire—round after round into the panic-stricken mob. Estimates of the dead ranged up to one thousand, with three or four times that many wounded. Moorhead Kennedy, the third-ranking foreign-service officer among the American hostages later taken in Iran, would remember the deep and startling vehemence of his captors' cynicism, how they looked back on the events at Jaleh Square and recalled that on that terrible occasion, despite all the horror and blood and systematic carnage, Jimmy Carter held firm in his support of the shah.

That was not all Carter did, of course. He issued a statement deploring the bloodbath, but both in that statement and in a personal telephone call to the shah, he reaffirmed the basic course of American policy. At that particular time it was probably impossible for Carter to do otherwise—to recognize at the moment that the massacre at Jaleh Square was a critical turning point in the history of Iran, an irrevocable transformation from unrest to revolution, with the inevitable result that America's only option may have been to pick a side.

Carter was not alone in his failure to see it. There were very few dissenters among the makers of U.S. policy. But in Carter's own

case, one reason for the failure is particularly poignant, for at the time of the massacre, he was immersed in the critical early stages of the peace talks at Camp David.

On September 7, 1978, only a matter of hours before the troops opened fire and the bodies began to fall in Jaleh Square, Carter had stared into the eyes of Anwar Sadat, physically blocking his path as the Egyptian president tried to break off the negotiations with Israel. Ten days later the peace agreement between the two nations became the greatest triumph of Jimmy Carter's presidency. But distracted as he was by the demands of Camp David, Carter gave Iran only secondary attention—precisely at the moment when far more was required.

Perhaps, however, the result would have been the same, even without the diversions of the Middle East, for Carter was committed to both imperatives of his Iranian policy—support for the shah and support for human rights—and he was determined to avoid the necessity of a choice. Later, after the tragedy was upon him, after the shah had fallen and the hostages were taken, Carter became by necessity far more decisive. His attentions, at last, were fully engaged, and he was no longer the victim of his own crowded agenda.

But even then, Gary Sick and others would argue, Carter served himself badly. He had a tendency to immerse himself totally in the substance of policy. In the words of James Fallows, Washington editor for the *Atlantic Monthly*, Carter was "often very good at figuring the right thing to do." But when it came to selling his decisions—packaging them in the rhetoric and symbols of the political marketplace—Carter seemed to lack the skill, the energy, or even the interest. "He seemed to believe," wrote Sick, "that if a decision was correct, it would sell itself."

That was seldom true in the ambiguous rough-and-tumble of American politics, and it certainly wasn't true in the case of the Iranian hostage crisis, where the most visible result was fourteen

months of frustration. And so, once again, Carter boxed himself in. Publicly and privately the crisis became his first priority, and the nation quickly sensed the depth of his concern. Slowly, however, the obsession raised a question: If he can't figure a way to accomplish his number one objective, what can he do?

Soon the second-guessing became more frequent and unforgiving: Carter should never have supported the shah of Iran; he should have supported the shah more fully. He should have resisted the temptation of a military rescue; he should have used greater force. He should tell the American people more about what's going on; he should try to shove the story off the media's agenda.

Carter, then as always, was philosophical about his critics: "It's easy to give advice," he said a little wanly.

For me, that ranged all the way from returning the Shah [from his exile in Panama] to be executed, to bombing Tehran with atomic weapons. I could have done either one. I could have destroyed Iran with one F15 air strike. I would have killed all the hostages, of course.

On the spur of the moment such a show of force might have been popular. I don't even know if that's an accurate statement. But I think in the long-range analysis of it, it would have been looked upon as a cowardly and inappropriate thing to do. So I never was really tempted.

We exhausted every possibility of securing the hostage release by diplomatic means, using the Libyans, the PLO, the Germans, the Japanese, everybody we could, plus our own direct—or rather indirect—influence, and it was not until the first part of April that our last effort with Bani Sadr and Ghotbzadeh fell through. We thought we had a deal worked out. In fact, we did, and it was countermanded by Khomeini.

And only then did we decide to move in another direction, which I thought would be successful. I'm still convinced that the rescue

mission was an excellent plan that had an outstanding chance of working.

The *New York Times* came out a month or two after I left office with a whole Sunday magazine devoted to the Iranian crisis. I read it very carefully. It's still in my files. There's not anything in there that advocates a tangible alternative to what I did, even with the benefit of two months of hindsight and analysis by experts on the subject.

We never were sure we were right, of course. How do you deal with fanatics who refuse to deal with you? We never knew from one day to another if Khomeini wouldn't command that a hostage be taken out every morning and executed at sunrise—publicly. We never knew what he was going to do.

So I sent him a message directly through the Swiss embassy and also through the leaders of Japan, West Germany, Great Britain, France and Italy, that if he put a hostage on trial, we would interrupt all commerce between Iran and the outside world. And if he killed or injured a hostage, we would take military action against Iran. And that's what I would have done.

It could have gone all the way from destroying the Iranian seaport facilities to destroying the ability to produce and refine oil. I would have avoided population centers. But if they had killed a hostage, I would have had to carry out my threats. And I would have.

So it was a very trying year, the worst year of my life, but it was a time for constraint and for valuing human life. And at the same time, it was necessary to protect the interests of my people and the integrity of our country. I never did feel that I had to prove that we had powerful military forces. That's a fact that's generally accepted. I think in the end the opinion of our country didn't suffer.

Having absorbed all of that, it is still possible to say, as the voters basically did in 1980, that in the final analysis results are what matter, and the results were not good: Iran fell to Khomeini. Fifty-two Americans were trapped in brutal circumstances for more than a

year. And Jimmy Carter couldn't find the means to alter either situation.

Five years after his departure from office, Carter didn't really quarrel with that interpretation. He understood what cost him his job, and few were more disappointed in the results than he was. And yet, for all of that, there was little he would change among the decisions he made—particularly among those after the hostages were taken.

James David Barber, the presidential scholar at Duke University, believed there were fundamental lessons in the Iranian ordeal, and for average Americans the main one was this: We tend to accord almost mystical properties to the office of the presidency and also to the person—the ordinary mortal—who happens to occupy it at any given time. Presidents personify our national aspirations, and as a result of that we tend to be irrational—entirely too extravagant in assigning credit when things go well or blame when they don't.

Barber's interest, meanwhile, was in presidential character. And the Iranian crisis, he said, was one of the most frustrating and demanding tests of that quality in the modern history of the presidency. Barber argued that Americans should assess Carter's handling of the crisis not by the standards of our national mythology but by what the episode really revealed about the nature of Jimmy Carter. Barber's implication seemed to be that by that standard, despite all the frustration and pain, there was no particular mystery about Carter's peace of mind.

Perspective in Plains

It was 1985, a Norman Rockwell scene on a Baptist Sunday morning in Plains, Georgia: the church nestled in a grove of pecan trees, and the cars, many of them symbols of small-town affluence, parked beneath the shade, filling the parking lot and spilling onto the lawn; across the road, a John Deere tractor, standing idle in a field of corn, its tires stained red, the chunks of Georgia clay still clinging to the treads.

The Reverend Dan Ariail arrived at nine-thirty. He was the minister at Maranatha Baptist, and he looked the part—stocky, red haired, with an easy smile and a generous disposition, greeting the visitors and trying to make them feel at home. Yes, he said, President Carter was scheduled to teach his class that morning, and yes, of course, everybody was welcome. And when the question came, as it inevitably did back in those days—What is it like to have a president in your church?—Ariail replied with a practiced sincerity: "Oh, it's fine, you know. To us around here, he's just Jimmy."

In fact, that assessment was only partly true. Carter may have been an active participant in the church, may have taught his Sunday school class every weekend he wasn't traveling, and he and Rosalynn may have vacuumed the sanctuary when their turn rolled around, but Jimmy Carter was not simply one of the boys down

in Plains. The other boys didn't have Secret Service agents hovering at their elbows; they didn't jet off now and again to Damascus, Buenos Aires, or Cairo; and none of them had ever greeted a group of former hostages at a Wiesbaden hospital or matched wills simultaneously with Menachem Begin and Anwar Sadat.

Those things and other memories separated Carter inevitably and profoundly from the place of his origins. Yet it was more than a matter of sentiment whenever he declared that Plains was home. Then as later, there was probably no other place where the nuances of his personality, or the subtlety of his values, were sketched with greater clarity.

Carter was capable of impatience and coldness, and those who worked with him through the years—Hamilton Jordan, Gerry Rafshoon—all came to dread the arctic chill of his displeasure. But as a matter of principle as well as inclination, Carter was more often friendly and unpretentious, and visitors to Plains in the 1980s found him quietly at ease with the richness of his memories and the vigorous challenges he had mapped for his future.

That contentment came as a surprise to many people. "Bitterness is the black beast that stalks politicians," Ray Jenkins, a former Carter aide once noted. "I have observed but few who managed to escape it. When you find an exception, almost always it's a religious person." In Carter's case interviewers consistently searched for the bitterness: anger at his critics, doubts about the things that didn't work out, frustrations from an agenda only partially complete. And there were, of course, times when Carter was angry—when he wondered what might have happened if Edward Kennedy's challenge hadn't lasted so long, or if there had been no crisis in the international price of oil, or if the helicopters had functioned in the deserts of Iran.

But Carter was also disdainful of living in the past. More than that, he was essentially incapable of it, for it was a violation of his values, as well as his nature. Although his Christianity may have

offered a measure of reassurance, a bedrock of certainty in a time of rapid change, it served also as an affront to satisfaction.

"The theologian Paul Tillich," Carter explained, pausing beside the lectern in his Sunday school class,

> wrote that religion is the search for the truth about our existence, our relationship with God, our relationship with others. It raises major questions that undermine our complacency: What is truth? What is wisdom, what is the nature of life, the essence of reward and punishment? What should we seek from God? What is the purpose of prayer? How much should we be concerned about ourselves?
>
> One preeminent theme in the teachings of Jesus is a warning against pride. Pride keeps our minds from being stretched, and when we think we know it all and are satisfied with what we have accomplished in the eyes of God, we are already far from God. Unless we are attempting things that might fail, we have too little faith in ourselves or in God.

For some people who visited his class in those days, all of that had the ring of mere homily—the tidy predictability of a Baptist Sunday school. For Carter, however, it was what he believed, and the proof seemed to be in the vigor of his life. Within a few months of his departure from Washington, he was thinking hard about what to do next.

Professionally, his primary focus would become the Carter Center—a nonprofit, public-policy institute founded by Carter in 1982 in partnership with Emory University. Located next to the Carter Presidential Library, on a wooded hill overlooking the Atlanta skyline, the center in the beginning assembled diplomats and scholars to discuss such subjects as the arms race or Middle East peace. At two of the largest early conferences Carter acted as co-host with former president Gerald Ford, a once-bitter rival who had become a friend, and their collaboration, implicitly, was a statement about America: that the things that unite it transcend divisions and that some issues are too important for partisanship.

In addition, Carter began to lecture when he chose—at Emory and other universities—and he began writing books that would include a novel on the Revolutionary War, a collection of poetry, and a primer on the politics of the Middle East. But perhaps Carter's most celebrated postpresidential activity, the one at the start that did the most to restore his public standing, was his affiliation with Habitat for Humanity, a nonprofit enterprise in Americus, Georgia, dedicated to providing decent housing for the poor.

Habitat was the ambitious undertaking of Millard Fuller, a tall and energetic former Alabamian who, in the 1960s, gave away his multimillion dollar financial empire because, he said, the pressures had become a threat to both his integrity and his marriage. In 1965 Fuller moved his family to Koinonia Farms, Clarence Jordan's interracial commune down the road from Americus, and he spent long hours absorbing Jordan's peculiar and haunting understanding of Christianity—a kind of radically literal interpretation of the Bible.

Once, for example, during Fuller's affiliation with Koinonia, a minister friend of Jordan's came calling with a problem: The janitor at the minister's church—a hard-working man with a wife and eight children—was compelled to subsist on eighty dollars a week. "It's wrong," the minister said. "I have pleaded with the deacons to raise his salary to a reasonable level, but they say we can't afford to; there's not enough money in the budget. What can I do?"

Jordan mused over the dilemma for a moment, then suggested a solution: Swap salaries with the janitor, he offered matter-of-factly. He pointed out that such a move wouldn't affect the size of the church budget and that the minister—with only two children instead of eight and with a comfortable place to live provided by the church—could subsist on eighty dollars more easily than the janitor. Sensing the minister's discomfort, Jordan demanded gently: "What's wrong, John? What's wrong with that solution? Is it contrary to Christian doctrine?"

Jimmy Carter, already aware of Koinonia Farms and serious enough in his own odysseys of the faith, was intrigued by Millard Fuller's telling of such stories—and even more so by Fuller's account of the origins of Habitat.

The idea took shape in discussions with Clarence Jordan—long, prayerful musings on Exodus 22:25: "If you lend money to any of My people who are poor among you, you shall not be like a moneylender to him; you shall not charge him interest." Applying the notion to low-income housing, Jordan and Fuller decided to build livable homes near Americus, relying on volunteer labor and—to cover the initial costs—donations and loans from the friends of Koinonia. The point was not to offer houses as charity but to sell them to the poor for exactly what they cost—no interest, no profit—and then to use the house payments to begin new construction.

Millard Fuller called it "the economics of Jesus," and in Jimmy Carter he found a willing disciple to the Habitat idea. First, it was a way to break the cycle of poverty—a concrete improvement in the lives of poor people but one they could take pride in the necessity of earning. But more than that, in the dozens of American cities and third-world countries where Habitat began to operate, it was a way to involve the affluent and the comfortable in a sacrificial gesture of Christian partnership.

"How many of us," Carter demanded of a Charlotte, North Carolina, audience in the summer of 1985, "have done something for other people that caused a real sacrifice for ourselves? One of the most disturbing things in the Bible was when Jesus declared late in life, 'Inasmuch as you have done it unto the least of these my brethren, you have done it unto me.' What that means is that as we are aware of hunger, homelessness and other human needs and do nothing about them, that is an expression of our actual attitude toward Jesus Christ." Carter was dressed, as he spoke, in a faded

work shirt and khaki pants that seemed out of place in the elevated pulpit of an affluent Charlotte church. But he made no apology, nor did the crowd seem to expect one, for he was on his way by chartered bus to the back streets of Harlem, where, for the second summer in a row, he was to serve as a volunteer builder of Habitat houses.

The task was one that he seemed to approach with relish, for in the eventful years since the end of his presidency, Carter had settled into the role of moral leader, a part that he never quite mastered as president but one that he had begun to play without the contaminating nuisance of day-to-day politics. "It's not a bad life," he said with a smile, and indeed it didn't seem to be. On a rainy afternoon in Plains, shortly before his 1985 trip to New York, he leaned back on a couch in what used to be his late mother's house—an unobtrusive brick building he was using for an office—and in a manner as casual as his striped work shirt and his faded blue jeans, he talked about his life at the age of sixty: "I did my best," he said of his presidency,

> and I think tangibly speaking we accomplished some good things. The standards that we set I think will be permanent. So I feel at ease with myself.
>
> The main thing now is for me to look to the future. Rosalynn and I are both relatively young (Rosalynn was then fifty-seven), and I'm now carving out a career that I hope will be as significant perhaps as my time at the White House.
>
> The Carter Center is where we will devote the rest of our active lives. We'll work on matters that are not surprising: peace throughout the world, the resolution of crises or disputes, the enhancement of human rights, arms control, environmental quality, health care, improvement in educational processes; trying to bridge the gap between ourselves and developing nations.

Carter said he saw his own agenda as essentially the antithesis of Ronald Reagan's. His successor, he said, had

abandoned and even opposed the civil rights movement in this country—and abandoned the human rights movement abroad.

There is obviously the ability of a president, particularly one as effective in the media as Reagan, to strengthen certain inclinations on the part of the American people. He makes it acceptable for those of us who are white, secure, prosperous and independent to assume that we're that way because we're especially worthy, or blessed by God—and that people who don't measure up to those standards are somehow inferior. It's their own fault that they're not as successful as we are.

That's been the very attractive contribution of Reagan to the sociological conceptions of our people. How long that can prevail, I don't know. It seems that for the first three or four months of his second term, it's begun to come apart. Whether that's just wishful thinking on my part, or whether it's actually taking place, I don't know.

I do know I never lost a vote of any significance in the House and Senate on matters concerning foreign policy and defense. My budgets on defense were never amended more than a half of one percent. Just fine adjustments. Recently, you see repeated revolutionary changes made in his major proposals. I don't know what this is going to portend for the future. It's hard to make a judgment.

But Carter understood that Reagan's occasional difficulties with Congress were largely overshadowed by an ironic truth: As president, Reagan touched something deep in the national psyche that Carter had not, and Carter's shortcomings had given him the chance. "Allowing Ronald Reagan to become president," he would admit years later, "was by far my biggest failure in office."

He knew also that he and Reagan would inevitably be compared, and in the end, he said, all he could do was let history be the judge. As Rosalynn Carter put it, a little wistfully perhaps, some four years after her husband left office, "Jimmy is secure in the fact that he did a good job. We assume that the record will be there for people to see . . . someday."

In fact, within a few years of Carter's defeat, people were already beginning to see it, but their judgments depended on ideology and perspective. Stuart Eizenstat, Carter's former chief adviser for domestic affairs, was convinced that Carter would be remembered as prophetic: a bold and independent president, part liberal and part conservative, ten years ahead of his time in charting a centrist course for the Democratic Party.

John Hope Franklin, the nation's most prominent African American historian, predicted Carter would "show up much better as time goes on. For one thing," said Franklin, "he was about as straight on the race question as we've ever seen in this country. He was committed to the concepts of bipartisanship and fairness. History will be hardest on him in terms of the day-to-day operation of government. But in terms of ability, foreign policy and the impulse to do the right thing, he'll be judged well."

Lee Atwater had a sharply different view. Before his death from a brain tumor in 1991 Atwater was a thirty-something Republican strategist from South Carolina and a major adviser for the 1984 Reagan-Bush campaign. Of the Carter administration, Atwater said: "It was a Chinese dinner presidency. It ended very quickly. I don't think people will remember it as a bad presidency. I just don't think there'll be any memory of it. In the twenty-first century, Carter will be regarded about like Millard Fillmore or Franklin Pierce."

Others, meanwhile, were part admirer, part critic. Hodding Carter, an outspoken Washington journalist who served as State Department spokesman during the Iranian hostage crisis, argued that Jimmy Carter (who is no relation) deserved major credit for his political courage and considerably less for his political skills. Said Hodding Carter of the president:

> He was willing to commit to some tough pieces of unfinished business, to press them forward. The Panama Canal treaty took more

capital than he probably could afford. He brought the same tenacity to Camp David, and someday, I trust that people will realize that it was a high water mark in the federal government's move toward openness.

His problems were implicit in the way he burst into the presidency. There were no Carterites. He didn't do enough to build a constituency, and he relied too much on an old and small circle. Deep down, he was suspicious of people who came to him and said, "Let me be a part." He spoke as if he were above politics and acted that way, too. But this is a political country. Washington is a political town, and thank God for it.

James David Barber, a political scientist at Duke University, suggested shortly after Carter left office that the competing assessments were likely to continue. Partly, said Barber, that's simply inherent in the way history is written. "You don't make your reputation as a historian," he explained, "by saying what the last guy said."

But as the years unfolded, Jimmy Carter seemed particularly susceptible to simultaneous strains of judgment. On the one hand, his idealism and integrity were essentially undisputed, and he accomplished a large percentage of a crowded agenda: the Camp David Accords, the pursuit of human rights, the Panama Canal treaty, SALT II, the normalization of relations with China, the deregulation of the private sector, an energy policy pushing conservation and alternative fuels. Carter was especially proud of his environmental record. Later, in his book *An Hour before Daylight*, he would write about his love of the land and about his boyhood life on a family farm in south Georgia. Such feelings and experiences, he said, underscored his resolve to triple U.S. wilderness reserves and double the size of the national park system. "Jimmy Carter is one of the two or three greatest environmental presidents in American history," contends Jay Hakes, a political scientist who later became director of the Carter Library.

On the other hand, as Carter himself understood, he never quite managed to translate his vision, to communicate in the symbols of the television age and explain himself effectively to 230 million Americans. That might not have mattered if his luck had held and 1980 had been a different kind of year. But his problems continued to grow, and Americans lost confidence in his ability to manage them.

For the next generation, the pendulum of perception continued to swing between those two realities—two competing sets of truth that defined the Carter presidential legacy. And yet another piece of truth, simpler perhaps, but every bit as durable, can be found in the words of James David Barber. "When an American president leaves office," he said, "with the Constitution more or less intact, and without a lot of dead American boys scattered around the planet, we ought to give him a medal."

The Carter Center

Carter was never very interested in medals, at least not as much as his critics seemed to think. There were always the doubters, the pundits who inevitably questioned his motives and speculated, among other things, that he was driven by the hunger for a Nobel Prize. Probably he should have won it already, back in 1978, when he faced off at Camp David with Menachem Begin and Anwar Sadat. Both Sadat and Begin had been awarded the prize on that occasion, but as anyone familiar with the summit would attest, the biggest step ever toward a Middle East peace would never have happened without Jimmy Carter. Yet the Nobel committee had made its decision, and as Carter continued his work through the years, his detractors insisted he was haunted by the snub.

In the *New York Times*, conservative columnist William Safire, giving voice to a view that was popular on the right, ridiculed Carter's "lust in his heart" for this greatest of all international awards. It was, argued Safire, what drove the former president on his assorted freelance missions for peace, some of which were at odds with U.S. policy. In December 1994, when a television reporter asked Carter about it, Carter immediately grew testy and dismissive. "What if the Nobel were the be-all and end-all of my existence?" he snapped. "And what if it never happened? Which

it probably won't. . . . What sort of a dried up, shriveled up, disappointed, frustrated old prune of a man would I be then?"

For the most part Jimmy Carter's colleagues found William Safire's notion absurd. Steve Hochman, for example, director of research at the Carter Center, had worked with Carter since 1981. When they first met, Hochman was a historian at the University of Virginia hired by Carter to help research the presidential memoir *Keeping Faith*. Hochman wasn't sure what to expect—perhaps a man caught up in the past, determined to defend his place in history, for that in part is the nature of a memoir. But what impressed Hochman most was Carter's fundamental obsession with the future, his need to make a difference and pursue his own agenda, which hadn't changed much since his days at the White House. "He was in a hurry to get the memoir done," remembered Hochman. "He was considering what to do with the rest of his life."

So even as Carter was working on his book, spending up to ten hours a day at the computer, his mind often took him in other directions. "He wanted," said Hochman, "to put together some kind of center" that could be the focal point of a whole new career. He was aware of the example of other ex-presidents—how Thomas Jefferson had founded the University of Virginia or John Quincy Adams had served in Congress and eloquently defended the cause of abolition. But Carter's ambitions took a very different form. He had no interest in political office, nor did he intend, in Hochman's view, to emulate any of the great men of the past.

Instead, he wanted to chart his own path, and he pursued his goals with an icy resolve, nurtured by the values he had held all his life. He seemed to be interested in more than a think tank. Even with the Carter Center's founding in 1982, after the first gatherings of scholars, politicians, and diplomats, when they would all come together to talk about the great trouble spots in the world, Carter seemed restless. He could certainly see the value of the brainstorm-

ing sessions, the blunt and constructive exchanges of perspective. But with civil wars raging in thirty different countries, the nuclear arms race beginning to reignite, and the world's poorest countries devastated by disease, Carter was eager to do something more.

For the next several years the Carter Center would struggle to find its identity. But Deanna Congilio, Carter's press secretary, sensed a breakthrough moment in 1989 when the center was asked to monitor elections in Panama. The country was close to Jimmy Carter's heart. As president he had endured his share of political risk in pursuit of the Panama Canal treaties. His article of faith had always been that the treaties themselves—and their message of respect for the people of Latin America—would be a step toward greater stability in the region.

The obstacle was General Manuel Noriega, the Panamanian strongman who had taken control of the country and had no intention of giving it up. But Carter, with the blessings of the first President Bush, had pressed Noriega to permit international monitoring of the May 7 vote. Carter himself would lead the delegation, along with former president Gerald Ford, a man he had long since come to admire.

For Carter it was more than a matter of rhetoric when, in his inaugural address, he had given Ford credit for "healing our land." Ford, after all, had had the courage to confront the country's central agonies. He had brought the troops home from Vietnam, and he had pardoned Richard Nixon, thus laying the Watergate scandal to rest. Carter understood that Ford had paid a price and respected the grace with which he had paid it.

Even so, their relationship had been chilly in the past, a residue of the 1976 election, when Carter had campaigned with characteristic self-righteousness, frequently using the word "disgrace" to describe Ford's policies for the country. Their feelings had warmed in a moment of tragedy. In October 1981 Egyptian president Anwar Sadat was murdered by fanatics, and the two ex-presidents

traveled to Cairo together for the funeral. On the long trip back they found time to talk, sharing, among other things, their sense of the magnitude of the loss. They called a press conference urging a stepped-up search for a Middle East peace. Two years later they wrote an article together criticizing Israel for failing to live up to the Camp David Accords, particularly with regard to Palestinian rights. In the years after that they would write other articles— supporting the equal rights amendment, criticizing the tobacco lobby—and would cohost international meetings on the arms race.

The trip to Panama was part of this pattern of cooperation. On this occasion, however, Carter would play the more prominent role. From the moment he arrived in the country, he exerted the force of his personality, confronting Noriega and his security forces in the streets, as gunfire rattled in the nearby towns. Many people had missed this side of Carter—certainly, for example, his critics on the right, who had regarded his foreign policy as timid, and many members of the media, who had seen him as a small, irresolute figure, given too often to changing his mind. Even many of his bedrock supporters were drawn to the softer, gentler side of his persona—the images of Carter on a Habitat project, embracing a new homeowner in Watts, telling her he was proud to work on her house. Almost nobody doubted the honesty of such an image, but to many Americans, the Jimmy Carter who monitored the elections in Panama was far less familiar.

This was the Carter of the Camp David summit—fearless, defiant, staring down a gaggle of Noriega's thugs, sustained by his righteous understanding of the truth. Indeed, there were moments when his Secret Service handlers feared for his life. But Carter was undeterred. In the end he would denounce the election as a fraud, winning admiration for himself in the process. Some critics on the right had feared his investment in Panama was so large that he would look at the country through rose-colored glasses and allow himself to be duped.

What happened instead was far more dramatic. On the day after the election, with stories of vote fraud sweeping through the country, Carter went down to the National Counting Center, where the election results were being tallied, and witnessed the massive ballot-stuffing for himself. After mounting a platform in the middle of the room, he shouted at the election workers in Spanish, "Are you honest or are you thieves?"

Carter said later that his indignation was rooted in sadness, for when he had negotiated the Panama Canal treaties with Noriega's predecessor, Omar Torrijos, they had talked about the two great aspirations of the Panamanian people. The first was the pride of sovereignty—an aspiration underscored by the treaties, which returned control of the canal to Panama—and the second was the shining promise of democracy.

But Torrijos had died in an airplane crash, and Noriega had assumed the mantle of power, ruling with a kind of ruthless corruption that offended Jimmy Carter to his core. Less than twenty-four hours after the election, with Noriega's forces controlling the streets, Carter called a press conference in his hotel lobby and condemned the dishonesty of the process. "I hope there will be a worldwide outcry," Carter declared, "against a dictator who stole this election from his own people."

Robert Pastor, Carter's top foreign-policy adviser for Latin America, observed the performance with a feeling close to awe. "It was Carter at his most impressive," said Pastor. "He was brilliant and eloquent. He walked through every step of the fraud, totally in control under tight and very bad circumstances. Noriega's chief of intelligence was standing next to me, and he said something like, 'You guys better get your asses out of here.'"

From the *Washington Times* on the right to the *Nation* and the *New Republic* on the left, the American media, once so critical of Carter and his style, were suddenly impressed by his physical courage and the personal force of his one-man diplomacy. From that point for-

ward, Manuel Noriega would become an international pariah, an election-stealing criminal, whose hold on his country would be short lived.

It was a breakthrough moment for the Carter Center, a foreshadowing of larger possibilities to come, and Carter immediately began to build on the triumph. Three months later Robert Pastor secured an invitation from Nicaragua to monitor its elections in 1990. Carter was delighted. For nearly a decade Nicaragua had been a flashpoint of dissension, a country wracked by civil war, which had become an issue in the United States as well. President Reagan, whose policies often drove Carter to distraction, had chosen Nicaragua as a place to draw the line against communism. He denounced the country's Sandinista revolution and the leftists who had taken control of the government and threw U.S. support behind a counterrevolutionary force called the Contras.

It was a policy that inflicted great pain on Nicaragua—with an economy in ruins and a war without any end in sight—but the country had known hard times in the past. For more than forty years it had lived in the grip of the Samoza dynasty, a father and two sons, brutal and greedy, who seemed to view Nicaragua as their personal estate. The Samozas fell in 1979, driven from power by left-wing rebels who had taken their name, the Sandinistas, from Augusto César Sandino, a revolutionary murdered in 1934 as the Samozas were consolidating their hold.

Jimmy Carter was president when the Sandinistas came to power, and his first response was to extend an olive branch. He pushed through Congress an eighty-million-dollar package of aid, despite growing fears in the United States that Nicaragua would become another Cuba. Carter warned the Sandinistas that the aid would be withdrawn if they tried to export their revolution to other countries, and he made clear his concerns about human rights. When Ronald Reagan was elected in 1980, running in part on a get-tough policy toward Latin America, the Sandinistas broke their

word to Carter and sent aid to leftist guerillas in El Salvador. In one of the final acts of his lame-duck presidency, Carter, in turn, cut off aid to Nicaragua.

The situation only grew worse for the next eight years, particularly for the Nicaraguan people. Late in the 1980s, however, there was a fragile hint of new possibilities. President George H. W. Bush, who succeeded Reagan in 1989, made clear that he wanted to defuse the Nicaraguan controversy, and the Sandinistas, still clinging to power, were eager to legitimize their regime.

The solution seemed to be a democratic election, and that was where Jimmy Carter stepped in. Fresh off his experience with Noriega, Carter agreed to monitor the Nicaraguan voting, believing the process could be free and fair.

Over the years, he had developed a feeling of mutual trust with Daniel Ortega, the president of Nicaragua and a leader in the Sandinista revolution. The breakthrough came in 1986, when Habitat for Humanity was building houses in northern Nicaragua, in an area known as Chinandega, and Carter was one of the Habitat volunteers.

He drove to the Habitat site with Ortega, a six-hour trip in Ortega's Land Rover along the pitted dirt roads of the Nicaraguan back country. "I had to sit and listen to his rhetoric," said Carter, "and I did." But Ortega did some listening also, and Robert Pastor, among other people, believed the Nicaraguan leader, more mature and politically astute than before, came to appreciate the risk that Carter had taken as president, pushing through the package of aid for Nicaragua. Whatever the case, Ortega had obviously reached the conclusion that Jimmy Carter now could be an ally.

As the 1990 election approached, Ortega was confident about the outcome, and he wanted the world to see it as legitimate. He knew that Carter had the kind of prestige to validate the result, and Carter, meanwhile, saw the chance for a step toward democracy. He wanted to do what he could to make it happen.

In Nicaragua he and his hard-working staff developed a plan they would soon use as a model for election monitoring all over the world. They came to the country six months before the vote and set up their own headquarters in Managua. The little democratic outpost would be led by Jennifer McCoy, a political scientist from Georgia State University. McCoy, long one of Carter's admirers, was impressed anew by the tenacity of his work. "He made five visits [to Nicaragua]," she said. "He is persistent. He can be stubborn."

Trusted essentially by both sides, Carter led negotiations before the election on a wide range of issues, including equal access to the Nicaraguan media and assurances that the vote would be secret. With the opening of the polls Carter was sure they had accomplished their objectives. He issued a statement in Spanish urging Nicaraguans to "be confident your vote will be secret and will count. We are here to make sure of that. . . . We will monitor every step of the process and do parallel vote counts to guarantee that the final results reflect the will of the people."

Robert Pastor, writing about the election several months later, was struck first of all by the size of the turnout—1.5 million people, more than 86 percent of the country's voters—but also by the mood of the crowd. For the most part they were somber and subdued, some of them looking around uncertainly, perhaps wondering what price they might have to pay. Arguably, this was the first free election in Nicaragua's history, and the roots of democracy did not run deep. But the people had reason to be hopeful also. In addition to Ortega, who had helped lead the Sandinistas' overthrow of Samoza, the other primary candidate for president was one of Nicaragua's most beloved citizens.

Violeta Chamorro was the widow of Pedro Joaquín Chamorro, a lifelong opponent of Samoza who was murdered in 1978. Initially a supporter of the Sandinista revolution, she had broken ranks in the early years and now led a diverse and sometimes fractured

opposition. She was a handsome woman with short gray hair and dark, steady eyes, and everybody knew she was a formidable candidate.

What stunned the Sandinistas was the fact that she won. The early counts left no doubt about it, and around midnight, after the polls had closed, Carter met quietly with Daniel Ortega. A few others from the Carter delegation were there as well—Elliot Richardson, former U.S. secretary of defense, who was a special envoy from the United Nations; Robert Pastor; and Secretary General João Baena Soares, of the Organization of American States. It was February 26, 1990, and Ortega's headquarters felt like a tomb, even with a rock band blaring outside. Pastor thought Ortega looked stricken. He was a thinnish man with thick dark hair and a drooping mustache, a little sad eyed in many of his pictures, and he seemed to be in a state of disbelief. He had worked so hard for the Sandinista revolution and had presided over a decade of war and a crumbling economy made worse by sanctions. It was nearly inconceivable to him that he'd lost.

Carter tried to be reassuring. He knew that Nicaragua was at a crossroads now, a moment of truth in which it could take a major step toward genuine democracy—or one in which Ortega could do what many a dictator had done in the past: find a pretext for overturning the elections. "In my opinion," Carter told Ortega, the Sandinistas

> can come out as heroes, having triumphed in a revolution against an oppressive dictator, survived a war against an enemy that was financed abroad, and at the end of ten years, brought democracy. . . .
>
> My feelings for you are very deep. Like you, I have won a presidential election, and I have lost one, but losing the election wasn't the end of the world. . . . If the world sees in you what I and others have seen, they will know you as a leader of pride, dignity and generosity. We are here to help you.

Clearly, this was Jimmy Carter at his best, direct and firm, but compassionate also, searching for the decency in Daniel Ortega. And in fact Carter found it. Ortega agreed to accept the results, and with Carter at his side, he paid a predawn visit to Chamorro to begin the peaceful transfer of power. For Carter, of course, there was irony in the moment. He had achieved as a citizen what he couldn't as president—a democratic Nicaragua that would soon be at peace, struggling with problems as deep and difficult as any in the region, but problems that at last seemed capable of being solved.

In the wake of Nicaragua, election monitoring became a staple of the Carter Center's work. In the next sixteen years Carter and his staff would oversee more than sixty elections in twenty-six countries, with many more on the way. In Peru and Palestine, in Mexico and Indonesia, and in many other places around the world, they carefully planted the democratic seed.

Sometimes it was dangerous and frustrating work. On election day in Guyana in 1992 Carter returned to the capital city of Georgetown after a poll-watching trip to the countryside to discover there were riots at election headquarters. The police attempted to whisk him away—somewhere, they said, out of range of the rock-throwing mob. Carter, however, would have none of it. "If there are riots at the election commission," he declared, "we are going there."

At the headquarters Carter confronted the people in the crowd, most of whom were angry because they had not been allowed to vote. "I investigated, as best I could, their allegations," he said. He also called the president of the country and the commissioner of police, and the violence in the end was tightly contained. But if it failed to undermine the election, it was a reflection of deeper problems in the country—the racial divide between citizens of African and East Indian descent.

Against that backdrop the Carter Center would spend another decade in Guyana, nurturing the fragile institutions of democracy. It also sought to do the same in Liberia. There, in 1997, Charles Taylor won a relatively open election, promising democracy but lapsing instead into a corrupt and brutal one-man rule. After Taylor was overthrown in 2003, the Carter Center returned to Liberia to monitor the 2005 elections. The winner this time was Ellen Johnson-Sirleaf, the first female head of state in Africa, and a long-time crusader for Liberian reform. A Harvard-educated former UN official, Johnson-Sirleaf promised an agenda of reconciliation for her war-torn country.

Nobody was certain how it would go. But that was often the case, said Deanna Congilio, Carter's press secretary, who had traveled frequently with him overseas: "It's two steps forward and one step back." But there had been enough progress over time to create a cautious sense of possibility in some of the most troubled countries in the world.

For Carter himself one of the great sources of satisfaction was the Carter Center's effort in the villages of China. He was proud of being the president who had finally normalized relations with China, and he used to say to the Chinese leaders that he felt his destiny and theirs were intertwined. Many of the Chinese officials felt the same, and they invited Carter to help monitor reforms in the countryside, where civil authority in many of the villages was strained almost to the point of collapse. In the midst of its massive economic reforms, China faced the problem of delivering local services—crime control, the collection of taxes and fees—in more than 650,000 small villages. Greater self-governance seemed to be the answer, and for practical reasons China began moving toward village democracy. Beginning with elections in 1998, the Carter Center began to monitor that process, working to ensure the transparency of the voting and then to train the new village officials. Yawei Liu, director of the Carter Center's China Project,

believed that within the first eight years the effect was beginning to spread to the cities. "It has begun to change the mindset," he said. "The initial motivation was not to become more democratic but to restore order and governance in the countryside. But now they [the Chinese leaders] can see how it works when you give people a choice."

As always, nobody was sure about the long-term effects. David Carroll, director of the Carter Center's Democracy Program, admitted that after more than fifteen years the results of the work were difficult to measure. Sometimes, he said, there were "unambiguous successes"—Mexico, Panama after the fall of Noriega—where the institutions of democracy had clearly taken root.

And of course Nicaragua. In 1990, on the night of Daniel Ortega's defeat, Carter had reminded him that he could run again—and Ortega did, three more times, finally winning in 2006, and promising to work with his opponents to build a better, more stable Nicaragua. "These are countries making halting progress," said David Carroll. "Nicaragua, Guyana, Mozambique." But in all of them, Carroll concluded, there's a new, if tentative sense of hope, a feeling that the strenuous effort is worth it.

As Robert Pastor put it, Carter and his staff have set an international standard for election monitoring and have helped to create in more than two dozen countries a climate where trusted elections could occur.

That, he said, is not a small piece of change.

Waging Peace, Fighting Disease

As the Carter Center continued to evolve, Carter was pleased with the way its mission was developing. In the beginning he had seen it as a kind of "mini Camp David," a place where people could come and talk—scholars, diplomats, world leaders—searching for a resolution to conflicts. Democracy building was more hands-on; it was "field work," as one staffer put it, and Carter couldn't have been more delighted.

It was a perfect match for his range of abilities that the people around him talked about with amazement. "He has the capacity to focus like a laser on an issue and try to drive it home," said David Carroll of the Democracy Program. "It's astonishing the degree to which his presence carries weight." But there was something else about Carter as well. He possessed an instinctive empathy, the ability not only to see both sides of a conflict but also, in his third-world travels, to identify on a visceral level with people in pain.

Once in Ghana in 1988, he and Rosalynn traveled from the capital city of Accra to a couple of villages not far away. One was Denchira, the other Elevanyo. The towns were dusty and hot in early March, just before the coming of the rains. Many of the villagers had left their thatched roof huts and assembled together in a little grove of trees. Most were afflicted with guinea worm, a waterborne pestilence dating back to early Egypt in which larvae grow

in the human bloodstream, blossoming into three-foot worms. Eventually they make their way to the surface, secreting a powerful acid that burns through the flesh. "It is like fire," one sufferer explained. "You feel it even unto your heart."

Many years later Carter would remember a beautiful young woman sitting apart from the rest, holding what seemed to be a baby in her arms. Carter and Rosalynn walked over to see her and discovered that what she was holding was not a baby but her breast, massively swollen with a guinea worm slowly emerging from the nipple. "I had to fight back nausea," Carter remembered.

Donald Hopkins, a Carter Center staffer in the village that day, remembers the Carters being "visibly shaken." Hopkins knew they had both heard of guinea worm before. Two years earlier an old Carter friend named Peter Bourne had come to Atlanta and shown Carter pictures of the guinea worm plague. Bourne had gotten his medical degree from Emory and then served as special assistant for health issues during Carter's term in the White House. Later he became assistant secretary general of the United Nations, where he directed a ten-year project to bring clean water to third-world countries. Bourne had seen his share of horrific diseases, and the irony was that many of them, including guinea worm, were relatively easy to control. What was needed was the political will—or perhaps more to the point, a person with the credibility and resources, as well as the stubbornness to stay with a cause that many people might consider quixotic. Bourne was sure that Carter was the man, and at their meeting in April 1986 he suggested a goal that he knew would be appealing. They would eradicate guinea worm from the face of the earth—a feat that had only happened one time, in the case of smallpox. Carter was intrigued and turned to Donald Hopkins to oversee the program.

Hopkins was a pediatrician by training and an epidemiologist as well, having worked at the Centers for Disease Control in Atlanta. He knew that Carter had the fund-raising gifts and the diplomatic

skills to deal with the leaders of the countries most affected, and he knew also, particularly after their visit to Ghana, that the disease touched Carter somewhere at his core.

Estimates were in the 1980s that there were 3.5 million cases in the world, with as many as 100 million people at risk. Most Americans had never heard of guinea worm, which didn't exist in North America or Europe, but which was a terrifying presence in many other places. In Nigeria there were 653,000 cases, in Ghana 180,000 more. There were epidemic numbers in Pakistan as well, and Hopkins decided to begin in those three countries.

His strategy included several approaches aimed at breaking the life cycle of the worm. The problem had to do with drinking water, particularly the small, stagnant ponds that so many third-world villages relied on. One alternative, of course, was a deep water well, drilling to a place where the water was pure. There were also cloth water filters donated by DuPont that the Carter Center distributed to thousands of families and a mild larvicide to put in the water—harmless to fish, plants, or people, but fatal to insects carrying the larvae.

By 2005 eleven of twenty countries where the Carter Center was working had eradicated the disease entirely, and the number of cases worldwide had dropped to just above ten thousand. In Nigeria where there was more to be done, there were only 120 known cases—down from more than 600,000 a few years before. That was the good news, Hopkins explained—a 99 percent eradication. The bad news was that it was easy to get complacent at such a point, especially among donors or third-world officials whose cooperation in the struggle was essential. And without a total eradication, Hopkins said, the disease, inexorably, would make a comeback.

In 2006 the *New York Times* published a series of articles on guinea worm and other plagues, describing the difficulties of the fight. Donald McNeil, author of the series, told the story of a Nigerian field officer in the guinea worm effort trying to locate the

source of the problem in a rural area known as Ogi. The official had heard rumors of a sacred pond said to be the place where the ancestors lived. The villagers used the pond for drinking water but refused to tell health officials where it was for fear of making the ancestors angry. When officials finally found the pond, the women of the village, chanting with rage, formed a human chain on the banks, refusing to allow the water to be treated.

That particular case was finally resolved. The water was treated. The worm disappeared. But in the remote and desolate back country of Africa, similar dramas took place every year, as Carter Center volunteers battled isolation and superstition—and perhaps also an ancient sense of defeat, a feeling that the worms were the punishment of God. "The last .3% is stubborn," said Carter, referring to the final cases in nine African countries. "They're in villages where people won't cooperate, or in a war zone. . . . This is a disease that afflicts the poorest, most isolated people in the world."

But whatever the level of frustration, he said, he shared with Hopkins a deep satisfaction, measured not only by the encouraging statistics but by the things the two of them had seen on the ground. As Hopkins put it, "It's really satisfying to go out to villages, and you see how hard the people work. For President Carter, it's almost visceral, maybe because he was a farmer himself. But to be able to help people see how to get rid of these terrible afflictions creates a sort of contagious energy, a sense of hope, that seems to spread to other parts of their lives. People realize they don't have to keep suffering."

As of 2006 guinea worm was one of five diseases the Carter Center was fighting. The others were river blindness, a fly-borne malady that the center had the goal of eradicating in the Americas; trachoma, a bacterial disease that has blinded more than 7 million people worldwide; lymphatic filariasis, which leads to a grotesque swelling of the limbs and affects as many as 120 million people; and schistosomiasis, a parasitic infection that attacks the bladder,

intestine, liver, and lungs, aiming its primary cruelty at children. In the latter three cases the Carter Center's goal was containment, not eradication, but in every case the work has been praised.

In 2006 the Bill and Melinda Gates Foundation presented the center with a one-million-dollar prize for "fighting the forgotten diseases," calling its efforts "extraordinary." But if such applause has been the norm for the health-care work of Carter, other pieces of his legacy have been more controversial. The critics, especially, have been aroused from their slumber when Carter has reentered the world of diplomacy.

In the summer of 1994 tensions were rising on the Korean peninsula. Carter had long had an interest in that part of the world. As president he had tried unsuccessfully to cut American troop levels in South Korea but couldn't muster the political support. For many years he had nursed an ambition to visit North Korea, and in fact he had a standing invitation. Kim Il Sung, the communist leader of that bellicose and isolated nation, had once called Carter a "man of justice" and for his own very complicated set of reasons seemed to be interested in developing a friendship. Carter, for his part, thought this was an area where he might do some good.

He had a deeply held belief in the value of dialogue, underscored powerfully by the Camp David summit. There he had seen two nations with a history of blood hatred—and two leaders who didn't particularly like each other—take historic steps toward peace. He knew dialogue didn't work every time, of course, but in the case of North Korea, he believed, Kim Il Sung had become a mythic figure, transformed almost to the status of a god by the people of his country and to the status of a devil by many others in the world, including policy makers in the United States. At the least, Carter was eager to see the man for himself, but he had deferred to the will of American presidents who did not want him to go. Early in the Clinton administration, however, tensions with Kim

were on the rise, centering on the issue of nuclear weapons, and some people were worried about the specter of war. One of those was James T. Laney, U.S. ambassador to South Korea.

Laney was the former president of Emory University, the place where the Carter Center began, and he and Jimmy Carter were close friends. A theologian by training, Laney was the kind of practical idealist that Carter admired, and the feeling was mutual. More and more in 1994 Laney was afraid that the Clinton administration's escalating hard line might lead to an accidental war—one that could easily result in a million casualties, including tens of thousands of U.S. soldiers.

Not that the administration policy was irrational. On the contrary, it involved a series of carefully calculated steps—pursuit of UN Security Council sanctions against North Korea; planning for a buildup of U.S. forces in the South; and eventually, if all else failed, consideration of a preemptive strike on the nuclear power plant at Yongbyon, where the government of Kim Il Sung was said to be pursuing the bomb.

The problem was that North Korea, a Stalinist throwback to the cold war era, had amassed a million-man army capable of overwhelming the thirty-seven thousand Americans stationed in the South, which might, in the end, require the unthinkable—the use of nuclear weapons against the North. That was the ultimate doomsday scenario, but even a conflict that fell short of that was a chilling possibility to many observers, Jimmy Carter among them. He was inclined to take the North Koreans at their word that UN sanctions would be a first step to war. And certainly he thought that the risk was insane without at least talking to Kim Il Sung.

Encouraged by the urgings of his friend Jim Laney, Carter sent word to President Clinton that he intended to accept North Korea's invitation to visit. His intermediary was Vice President Al Gore, with whom Carter had a good relationship. Gore agreed to intercede on Carter's behalf, seeking Clinton's blessing, if Carter

would simply tone down his request—telling Clinton he was "inclined" to go, rather than bluntly stating that he would. Carter agreed, and Clinton gave his approval, reminding Carter that he was making the trip as a private citizen, not an official representative of the government.

Many in the administration were worried. They understood Carter's dovish reputation, his opposition four years earlier to the First Gulf War, against Saddam Hussein—a policy that was widely viewed as successful. They also knew that Carter was stubborn and difficult to rein in when, as one of the Clinton people put it, "he got the policy bit in his teeth." In the end, however, Clinton thought the risk worth taking—such a mission might give Kim Il Sung a face-saving way to back away from the brink. Clinton understood that Carter's prestige in many corners of the world was hard to overstate. As the Carter Center's David Carroll put it, "It's double or triple the respect he receives in the United States. In many places, he's revered." For Kim Il Sung, considered by many to be an international rogue, merely having Jimmy Carter in his country would be a diplomatic coup.

Carter, meanwhile, understood the enormity of the stakes. With his small delegation he set out for Korea, arriving in Seoul on the afternoon of June 13, 1994. As usual, he was traveling with Rosalynn, his wife, who had been a full partner in most of his work, and Nancy Konigsmark, his long-time assistant, who handled her duties with efficiency and grace. In addition to their Secret Service detail they were joined this time by Marion Creekmore, a career diplomat who had left the Foreign Service in 1993 after serving as U.S. ambassador to Sri Lanka. Creekmore had accepted a position as program director at the Carter Center and in that capacity had helped to coordinate the details of the trip.

When the group met first with South Korean president Kim Young Sam, Creekmore was impressed by the diplomatic chill. The South Koreans didn't want Carter to go. They feared the manip-

ulations of Kim Il Sung, the possibility that he would simply use the Carter visit as a cover, a stalling mechanism while he continued to pursue his nuclear ambitions. The other thing Creekmore noticed was that Seoul was awash in preparations for war. The North Koreans had insisted all along that UN sanctions, which the United States was pursuing, would be seen as a declaration of war and that Seoul would soon become "a sea of fire." In this bustling capital of ten million people citizens everywhere were stocking up on food, and there were civil defense drills on Monday afternoon, the day Carter arrived, and again on Wednesday, as he was leaving for the North.

The tension mounted as his delegation crossed the DMZ, the demilitarized zone separating the North from the South. Only a handful of westerners had ever made that crossing, and none had been allowed to make it both ways. With their North Korean hosts Carter and the others drove for two hours on a nearly deserted four-lane highway through a flat or sometimes rolling landscape that was dotted with farms and little clumps of trees. "It was very pretty," remembered Creekmore.

That afternoon in the North Korean capital of Pyongyang, Carter met with Foreign Minister Kim Yong Nam, a stiffly polite hard-liner who seemed to offer little hope of progress. He reiterated the possibility of war and said the North Koreans were ready. "He was polite but very, very tough," said Creekmore. "That led Carter and the rest of us to wonder what the next day would bring."

As was his habit, Carter rose early on the following morning, June 16, and made final preparations for the meeting just ahead. He could only hope that Kim Yong Nam, the foreign minister, was North Korea's bad cop, and that Kim Il Sung would play the other role. And that, in fact, was how it turned out. North Korea's Great Leader, as he was known to his people, greeted Carter with a smile, declaring that trust was the most important thing. He was an impressive man even in his eighties, his hair still thick and only

partly gray, his mind still penetrating and sharp. He agreed early on that inspectors from the International Atomic Energy Agency could remain in his country, with all necessary access to his nuclear power plant at Yongbyon.

That was a critical point for the United States. But Carter pushed also for Kim to freeze his nuclear program—no refueling of reactors, no building of new ones—until official talks with the United States could begin. The Great Leader agreed on that point as well, asking for a pledge in return from the United States that it would refrain from attacking his country. He asked also for U.S. assistance in securing light-water reactors—a nuclear technology less capable of producing plutonium, the material that could then be converted to bombs. And finally he wanted shipments of fuel oil that could replace the lost energy from the plant at Yongbyon.

Before his trip Carter had been briefed by Robert Gallucci, assistant secretary of state, on the basic parameters of U.S. policy. Carter was certain that within that framework he and Kim had a deal that the Clinton administration could accept. He began to worry, however, that afternoon when he met with a team of North Korean nuclear experts who immediately tried to back away from the agreement. "Are you contradicting the Great Leader's policy?" Carter demanded, and temporarily, at least, the experts retreated. But fearing that his efforts could unravel, Carter decided that evening to do an interview with CNN, detailing the North Korean promises and forcing, he hoped, policy makers on all sides to back away from the brink. It was a bold and controversial move, an act of hubris, many critics thought, in which Jimmy Carter made himself the instrument of his own foreign policy.

Certainly the Clinton administration was annoyed, feeling boxed in, unable to move as freely because of Carter's television diplomacy. It was what many of the president's advisers had been afraid of—Carter charging off in his own direction, standing before the cameras and announcing that a peace deal had been made.

As far as the administration was concerned, there was a long way to go before that was the case, for the agreement so far was still unofficial, and nobody was sure that Kim Il Sung's word could be trusted.

Still, things were clearly much better than before and seemed to improve even more the following morning when the Carters joined the Great Leader and his wife for a three-hour cruise on the Taedong River. As Rosalynn Carter remembered it later, they passed through industrialized countryside that appeared very different from the beauty of Pyongyang, where roses grew on every hillside. Kim Il Sung was in rare form, pointing out the sights, boasting about his country's engineering feats, clearly enjoying the time with his guests. Jimmy Carter, however, had a larger agenda. As the cruise wore on, he and Kim rode the glass elevator to the second-floor deck of Kim's massive yacht, and there Carter pushed hard on two other points. He urged Kim to allow U.S.–North Korean teams to recover the remains of U.S. servicemen killed years earlier in the Korean War. And he argued strongly that the time had arrived for a high-level summit between North Korea and the South. Kim eventually agreed on both points.

As Rosalynn Carter noted later, her husband had accomplished everything he had hoped. He was exhausted now and let down his guard, and perhaps that is why he soon made the biggest blunder of the trip. With CNN recording the scene he assured Kim Il Sung that the United States was no longer seeking sanctions from the United Nations. It was not true. Though the Clinton administration now saw an opening for high-level talks, it was not yet ready to back away from sanctions. The president's advisers still believed in the need for such a threat.

Carter understood that, and later in his conversation with Kim he made clear that the notion for abandoning the sanctions was his own—a path he was prepared to urge on the president. But from the Clinton perspective the damage was done, for there was

Carter on CNN flatly misstating the government's position. Understandably, when the mission was over, the administration gave Carter mixed reviews. Many in policy-making positions viewed him as both headstrong and sloppy. Conservative commentators were even more harsh. Carter, they said, had chosen to "coddle" a communist dictator, and Charles Krauthammer of the *Washington Post* compared Carter to Great Britain's Neville Chamberlain, infamous for his appeasement of Adolph Hitler.

But despite the initial spasm of rhetoric, as the hysteria slowly began to subside, it was obvious that Carter had accomplished a breakthrough, pulling the world back from the precipice of war. It was Clinton himself, as much as anyone else, who started the swing of opinion back to Carter. "I was glad he went," Clinton told the media shortly after the mission, "and I thought it was a trip worth taking." Those close to the drama were far more emphatic. Marion Creekmore, who was part of the mission, and Ambassador Jim Laney, who had urged Carter to undertake it, both thought he had probably saved the world from a war—not a skirmish with a few hundred casualties, but a conflagration where a million people might have died. More concretely and far easier to prove, Carter had worked out with the North Koreans a set of understandings that would put their nuclear program on hold.

In the coming months the Clinton administration followed up skillfully on Carter's accomplishment, negotiating an official framework that stopped plutonium production in the North. The heart of the agreement would hold for eight years, until President George W. Bush, in the wake of the terrorist attacks of 9/11, would change the direction of U.S. policy.

As far as Ambassador Laney was concerned, the diplomatic breakthrough of 1994 was rooted in the strength and skill of Jimmy Carter. "His capacity to simply be determined and stubborn and absolutely unshakable resulted in an agreement," Laney said. "Without Carter, the likelihood that we would have crossed the

line was extremely high. But now it looked like a different day dawning."

Carter, meanwhile, regarded the Korean mission as a "miracle"—a harrowing test of his personal adage that "the possibility of failure is an acceptable risk."

The test would not be his last in 1994.

Barely three months later Carter found himself in Haiti, this time as an official emissary of his government. For several years Haiti had been a nation in crisis. Desperately poor and accustomed to ruthless dictatorial oppression, it had experienced at least a few months of hope, beginning in December 1990, when Jean-Bertrand Aristide was overwhelmingly elected as the nation's president.

But seven months later Aristide, the charismatic champion of the country's poor, was overthrown in a military coup. For the next three years the Bush and Clinton administrations stepped up pressure on General Raoul Cedras, the Haitian strongman who replaced Aristide. Cedras, however, had remained defiant and in the summer of 1994, faced with a flood of Haitian refugees, the United States secured a UN resolution allowing an invasion to reinstate Aristide.

By September thirty thousand U.S. troops were poised and ready to descend on the island. In the final hours before that invasion Clinton sent Carter, along with General Colin Powell and Georgia's U.S. senator Sam Nunn, to try to persuade Cedras to resign. Though Cedras officially had welcomed their coming, hoping apparently to stall or save face, the atmosphere was tense when the delegation arrived in Port au Prince. The National Military Headquarters, where Cedras was waiting, was surrounded by a mob of his supporters—at least a thousand machete-wielding Haitians. In Cedras's office inside the building, machine guns were leaning against the walls—a nerve-rattling display, especially with para-

troopers waiting to invade. "Carter hardly flinched," remembered Robert Pastor, who was also there to assist the delegation.

Pastor had seen his share of tight spots before. As Carter's top Latin American hand, he had been roughed up by Noriega's thugs in Panama and had traveled to some of the most volatile countries in the world. A Harvard PhD, he had also been a Peace Corps volunteer and later a National Security adviser when Carter was in the White House. Even in those days he regarded Carter as the calm at the center of the storm, almost serene amid the chaos around him, and once again in Haiti that seemed to be the case.

With the able participation of Powell and Nunn, Carter turned up the negotiating heat. The three envoys informed Cedras that an invasion was certain if he didn't step aside, and the American force would be overwhelming. From there the discussion centered on details, but the progress was slow, and no agreement was reached until after the invasion forces from the Eighty-second Airborne had left their base in North Carolina. It was a frantic, last-minute piece of diplomacy in which the Carter team secured an agreement for the resignation of Cedras, the peaceful arrival of U.S. forces, and the return of Aristide on October 15.

Three months after his Haitian mission Carter closed out the year by flying to Bosnia and to the war-ravaged streets of Sarajevo to negotiate a cease-fire between Muslims and Serbs. In the end the truce didn't hold, but at least it offered a small hint of progress, and Rosalynn Carter, among many others, thought it had been a good year for peace. She wondered if her husband would win the ultimate prize for his efforts. In 1978 he had been passed over for the Nobel after he had brokered, almost single handedly, the Camp David Accords between Egypt and Israel. Now in 1994 he had saved the world from a war in Korea and Haiti from a U.S. invasion and had helped to restore the latter country's fragile democracy.

That was how Mrs. Carter saw it, and she was dismayed when the Nobel committee chose another winner. In 1995, the year after

Carter's diplomatic successes, it was Joseph Rotblat, a British nuclear physicist who had long campaigned against nuclear weapons. He was, like most of the Nobel laureates, a commendable choice, one of many citizens of the world who had committed themselves to the ideal of peace. As Carter told James Wooten of ABC News, "There are so many hundreds of people working for the same things, just as hard as I am and some of them probably much harder."

And so, according to Rosalynn Carter, she and her family decided not to worry about the prize any more. "We decided it was never going to happen," she said. And that was all right. Jimmy, she explained, would simply move ahead with his work.

Endangered Values

Sometimes Carter skated where the ice was thin.

In his book *The Unfinished Presidency* historian Douglas Brinkley tells of a trip that Carter made to Nigeria. In March 1995 the former president was in Africa on one of many visits to call attention to the guinea worm problem. He and Rosalynn decided to travel to the village of Enugu, where many people were suffering from the disease, and the Carters were treated quite literally as saviors. Amid the flood of good will Nigeria's head of state Sani Abacha acceded to a Carter request that he free a prominent political prisoner.

It was something that Carter had done quite often, putting personal pressure on the world's dictators to improve their performance on human rights. General Abacha was one of the worst, but he was nobody's fool. He was delighted when Carter chose to publicize clemency for the prisoner, for it created the appearance of human rights progress. Back in the United States, Nigerian dissident Wole Soyinka, a Nobel laureate, delivered a speech at the University of Georgia denouncing Carter for his "extremely harmful naiveté." Carter ruefully admitted his mistake in giving legitimacy to General Abacha. A few months later the Nigerian strongman hanged nine dissidents in a display of his power. Such were the brutal realities of Africa.

Still, Carter thought progress was being made, for as terrible

as the man-made atrocities might be—the ravages of political oppression and war—the casualties of famine and disease were even worse. On that front there were clear signs of hope: a sharp reduction in the guinea worm plague and progress in the battle against river blindness. In 1995 the Carters made five trips to Africa, where they saw firsthand the effects of Mectizan, an antibiotic donated by Merck, and the increasing productivity of small farms—the result, in large measure, of the Carter Center's agricultural programs.

The center by now had developed momentum, a full and expanding sense of its mission. It was on its way to training more than four million farmers on the continent of Africa, and in its first twenty years it would monitor forty-four elections in twenty-two countries. By 2002 seven countries in Africa and Asia had completely eliminated guinea worm, and the Carter Center had forged alliances with the Centers for Disease Control in Atlanta, UNICEF, and the World Health Organization to continue the fight against other epidemics. In Africa and Latin America combined, the center would deliver more than forty million treatments for river blindness.

Much of the work occurred with little fanfare, though every now and then Carter's personal travels would be met with international headlines—and on scattered occasions, a full-fledged frenzy of media attention. That had certainly been the case in 1994, with his missions to Haiti and North Korea, and it happened again in 2002 when Carter paid a visit to the island of Cuba.

He had wanted to take the trip for a while, and two years earlier at the funeral of Canadian prime minister Pierre Trudeau, Fidel Castro had invited him to come. The idea was first discussed in 1995 when Robert Pastor, representing the Carter Center, met with Castro for more than seven hours, which, as Pastor noted, was not especially unusual. The Cuban dictator was always a talker. Carter was looking forward to his own conversations, but perhaps even more, he wanted to talk to ordinary Cubans—to express his hopes

for better relations and, far more delicately, from Castro's perspective, to talk about democracy and human rights. Even as president, Carter had hoped to normalize relations with Cuba, but the hopes fell victim to Cuba's military intervention in Africa. More than twenty years had passed since then, and the official hostility was still just as strong. Carter hoped to do what he could.

Logistics for the trip were placed in the hands of Jennifer McCoy, the veteran Carter Center staff member who had headed the field office in Nicaragua for the historic 1990 election. McCoy discovered that she loved the work. Although she had been a political scientist at Georgia State University, nothing in her classrooms or in the pages of books was quite as exciting as her real-world experience with Jimmy Carter. She was deeply impressed by the man himself—his steel-trap mind, his almost staggering level of energy, his tunnel-vision insistence on doing whatever he thought was right.

In the case of Cuba that meant talking to everybody he could. Before the trip he met with Cuban American leaders, bitterly opposed to the Castro regime, and when he got to the island, he insisted on talking to political dissidents. Even more dramatically he made a televised speech to the Cuban people, delivered live and in Spanish with no censorship by the Cuban government. Carter called for an end to the U.S. embargo of Cuba, which he said inflicted pain on the Cuban population. But he also called for Fidel Castro to respect human rights and to institute an open democracy for his citizens. In many ways it was vintage Jimmy Carter—searching defiantly for some middle ground, challenging the prevailing assumptions around him, regardless of whom he might offend in the process. "It took some discussion," remembered McCoy, for the Cuban government to allow such a speech. "They did not know what he would say."

By all accounts Carter took personal delight in the moment, just as he did in his other Cuban stops. In Havana he visited a

school for disabled children, who put on a song-and-dance show, and there was a trip to a Cuban health-care clinic, where members of the Carter delegation were able to assess a part of the Cuban experience that was working. In addition to that, Carter enjoyed his meetings with Fidel Castro, who treated the former president with respect. Castro ordinarily was something of a night owl, with dinner meetings lasting until 3 a.m., while Carter, the peanut farmer from Georgia, was early to bed, early to rise. "We kept noticing," said Rosalynn Carter, "that he was kind of hurrying through what he had to say. We asked him about it, and he said, 'Well, I know you like to go to bed before twelve.'"

What the visit accomplished is hard to say. Two days later, President George W. Bush clamped down further on travel restrictions to Cuba, a calculated gesture of official hostility, and the following year Castro cracked down on political opposition, arresting seventy-five dissidents and sending them to jail. Officially, noted Jennifer McCoy, nothing much changed. Nevertheless, it was a triumphant moment for Carter himself. The visit to Cuba, the first by a U.S. president since the Cuban revolution, was covered by more than three hundred media, most of whom gave Carter good reviews. For the most part Cuban American leaders were also pleased. Carter, they said, had been straight with Fidel, which they were happy to see.

Coming in May 2002, the Cuba trip also served to highlight the twentieth anniversary of the Carter Center. The center now had a permanent staff of more than 150 people, with volunteers in every corner of the world, and in the international arena of NGOS—nongovernmental organizations—Carter and his coworkers had helped set the standard. Taken together, the anniversary and the visit with Castro began to resurrect an old, familiar question. Would Jimmy Carter finally win the Nobel Prize?

As the Nobel committee neared its decision, the Associated Press ran a speculation story that Carter indeed was on the short

list. Carter and Rosalynn didn't pay much attention. They had heard it before, and there was work to be done. Even on the night before the announcement, October 10, 2002, they went to bed early, unaware of what was coming. "We didn't even know that this was the day," remembered Mrs. Carter, "much less that Jimmy would win." But at four the next morning, the telephone rang and the Secret Service agent gave them the news. "Jimmy!" Mrs. Carter screamed with excitement, and the two of them knew busy times were ahead.

Meanwhile Deanna Congilio had been awake for two hours. As the Carters' press secretary she had received strong hints from Norwegian television that she ought to be prepared, and by five that morning National Public Radio was calling. Twenty minutes later when she came to her office, her voice-mail box was already full. Soon the letters began to pour in. "Dear Jimmy," wrote the first President Bush, a man whose gracefulness Carter had admired, "Congratulations! Barbara and I [are] so very pleased at the enormous good sense shown by the Nobel Peace Prize committee." And the great Jewish author and holocaust survivor Elie Wiesel, already a Nobel laureate himself, scrawled off a note that came from his heart: "Dear President Carter and friend, I just heard the good news at long last."

For its part the Nobel committee conceded in its formal announcement that Carter could easily have won much earlier. The committee cited the Camp David Accords, "in itself a great enough achievement to qualify for the Nobel Peace Prize," and also mentioned the Carter Center's work on disease and human rights. But perhaps the clearest hint about the timing of the prize came in a paragraph directly about peace, contrasting Carter with the world's saber rattlers who were even then turning up the volume of conflict and war.

At the Nobel ceremony on December 10 Carter set out to address those themes. He paid tribute to the Nobel winners of the

past—to Anwar Sadat and Yitzhak Rabin, heroes and martyrs in the cause of peace; to Mikhail Gorbachev, who decided it was time to end the cold war; and to Martin Luther King Jr., "the greatest leader my native state has ever produced." "I have witnessed the capacity of destitute people to persevere under heartbreaking conditions," Carter said in his speech.

> I have come to admire their judgment and wisdom, their courage and faith, and their awesome accomplishments when given the chance to use their innate abilities.
>
> But tragically in the industrialized world, there is a terrible absence of understanding or concern about those who are enduring lives of despair and hopelessness. We have not yet made the commitment to share with others an appreciable part of our excessive wealth.

And on the subject of war, which seemed to be looming as America was preparing to invade Iraq, Carter concluded his talk by proclaiming: "War may sometimes be a necessary evil. But no matter how necessary, it is always an evil, never a good. We will not learn how to live together in peace by killing each other's children."

Out in the audience, Rosalynn Carter listened to his words, remembering the journey the two of them had made. "Of course it was a thrill," she acknowledged sometime after the ceremony was over. And later she added with characteristic candor, reflecting on the honor her husband had received, "I thought he deserved it."

In a 2006 interview Mrs. Carter was asked what the highlights were, the most memorable moments from the Carter Center's work, which the two of them had shared so fully. She mentioned the North Korea trip, the visit with Fidel, and the monitoring of all the historic elections. She talked also about her work on mental health, work that had been uniquely her own, but perhaps the most satisfying of all had been the heartening battle against third-world

disease. They had seen the horrific cases of suffering, but they had also seen the birth of new hope, the symptoms of healing, as isolated villagers took control of their lives. "It does something to your heart," she said.

Given all of that, and with her husband turning eighty in 2004, some wondered if the couple would be slowing down. Mrs. Carter knew this was not Jimmy's way. He still had his store of restless energy and his technocratic focus, the ability to concentrate on any task at hand. These qualities were there in his work, as well as in his avocations and hobbies—the hours spent in his woodworking shop or in restoring the old inn in downtown Plains.

They were also present in his work as a writer. He had written twenty books by 2005 on a wide array of topics, including the presidency, the environment, and his Christian faith. He had written a children's book with Amy, his daughter, and in 2003 he became the first ex-president to write a novel. He also tried his hand at poetry, traveling to Arkansas to see his friend Miller Williams, a poet of international renown.

Williams, who had delivered the second inaugural poem for President Bill Clinton (and who was also known as the father of country singer Lucinda Williams), remembered the Carter visit well. The former president, he said, came to Fayetteville and spent three days at the Williams home, talking poetry over coffee and wine and absorbing in a concentrated time what it took Williams's students a semester to learn. "I was impressed," Williams said, "by what good use he made of the time, and what he was able to pick up quickly. As a poet, he is well worth reading. All his poems begin as Jimmy Carter's and end as the reader's. That's the line, I think, between an amateur and a more serious poet."

But whatever the satisfactions of his hobbies Carter at heart was still a politician, still a citizen of a troubled world, and even his writing reflected that fact. His twentieth book, published soon after his eightieth birthday, examined what he called "Our Endan-

gered Values," principles with roots running deep in his faith. To Carter these were conservative values, time honored and revered, but oddly enough, as he understood it, they were under attack from the political right. In his book and in his other public pronouncements Carter did his best to take a stand against what he saw as a new force in America: a religious movement intertwined with politics that he had come to regard as a national tragedy.

Part of his critique was political, reflecting a sharp disagreement with President George W. Bush. Whether the issue was drilling for oil in northern Alaska or waging preemptive war against Iraq, Carter thought Bush had drifted off track, perhaps as far as any president he could name. But Carter's concerns were much broader. He was worried also about a politicized fundamentalist crusade that saw the world in stark black and white and that selectively elevated certain parts of the Bible—sometimes from obscurity—to the top spot in its hierarchy of sins.

A case in point was homosexuality, a phobia exploited by Bush in his run for reelection. As Carter noted, Jesus himself had never mentioned the subject, not even once, according to the gospels, and certainly within the Bible as a whole it was given far less attention than adultery or divorce. But suddenly in the religious politics of America, homosexuality was the most heinous sin, and that both puzzled and offended Jimmy Carter. In his book and in his Sunday school classes in Plains he proclaimed a Christianity of forgiveness, not a message of spite. "Judge not, that ye be not judged." It was always one of his favorite verses, along with dozens of others about the needy and the poor and the prophetic cry for justice in the world.

For Carter the Christian, it was a measure of some embarrassment and shame that his own country, the richest on earth, was also the stingiest when its philanthropy was measured against gross national income. In *Our Endangered Values* Carter returned to one of the themes of his Nobel address—how the growing disparity

between rich and poor, both among nations and within them, was the world's greatest threat to stability and peace.

With a passion rooted in the warmth of his faith but delivered in a style that was chilly and relentless, Carter argued that the Bush administration, supported by its conservative Christian allies, was making things worse. On issues such as the use of torture, the public condemnation of gays, and the massive disregard for the environment, Carter was appalled by the damage being done— and by the deep divisions being sown in the country. "I am right and worthy, but you are wrong and condemned." That, in Carter's view, was the disturbing message of the new Christian right.

The irony was that Carter himself had helped unleash the conservative Christian involvement in politics. Running for president in 1976, he had talked freely about his Christian faith in a way that was heartening to evangelicals. They had rarely heard anybody quite like him. In his book *With God on Our Side* historian William Martin argued that when Carter unapologetically, almost offhandedly, referred to himself as "born again," the national press didn't know how to take it. But thousands of Americans understood the statement completely, and regardless of their denomination or race they found it easy to get caught in the moment, when Carter accepted the Democratic nomination at a convention that suddenly felt like a revival.

Part of that feeling was the rush of reconciliation, as Martin Luther King Sr., whose son was murdered for the cause of civil rights, took the stage with Carter—two Georgians, one black, one white, reaching out across the great divide. But there was more to it than that. There was also the rush of religious fervor as the Reverend King closed his eyes to pray and declared with the passion that had long been his trademark, "Surely the Lord is in this place."

As the campaign developed momentum, the media was compelled to take Carter seriously—and by extension, the faith of

some of his new Christian followers. As William Martin wrote, when "it became clear that a Baptist Sunday-school teacher might actually be elected president, evangelical Christians received increased and more respectful attention."

It didn't take long, however, before the marriage between Carter and the evangelicals began to turn sour. Some of the strains were inevitable, the result of disagreements on issues. Carter supported the equal rights amendment, which many conservative Christians opposed, and although he shared their opposition to abortion, he supported the legality of *Roe v. Wade*. But historian John Turner of the University of South Alabama also argued that Carter turned his back on this new constituency in a way that is difficult to explain. Consistently after he was elected to the presidency, Carter turned down invitations to speak to the National Association of Religious Broadcasters, who held their annual meetings in Washington. Robert Maddox, a Carter adviser, thought it was a "tactical mistake" and was moved to wonder what might have happened if Carter had chosen to address face-to-face the evangelicals' steady drift to the right. Would it have made any difference? Could Carter have altered their political priorities? In retrospect nobody could say, but at one 1980 meeting he finally delivered an address to the Christian broadcasters and invited a few of them to the White House.

By most accounts the encounter with Jerry Falwell, Jim Bakker, and others was difficult. But when it was over, Bakker, one of the most politically moderate of the group, said he was moved by Carter's sincerity. "It's easier to take potshots at the image on the screen," Bakker said, "than it is when you're in the same room with a warm, decent man confessing his faith in Jesus Christ." According to one of his closest associates Bakker later voted for Carter, not Reagan, but among evangelicals he was in a minority. Whether it was Carter's reserve—his curious disdain among the ranks of

politicians for selling himself and his political ideas—or whether it was the inevitable clash of worldviews, the new Christian activists began to drift away.

They found new allies in the Republican Party, and a quarter century later Carter was offended by their agenda. He spoke out against it in the name of his faith but also, he said, in the name of his country. "There is obviously a widespread, carefully planned, and unapologetic crusade," he wrote, "under way from both sides to merge fundamentalist Christians with the right wing of the Republican Party." In the end, he argued, it was a deliberate attack on "the wall of separation" between church and state.

Some critics, even outside the Republican right, thought that Carter had gone too far, believing that in his writings and in other public statements, he had squandered a part of his elder statesman status by allowing himself to become partisan and shrill. Even his backers found it hard to deny that Carter was a man who still had an edge. But others like his fellow Baptist Will Campbell, a southern author and human rights advocate, believed that Carter had assumed a unique role in American life, one that very few others could play. "He's a prophet," said Campbell, "and we don't have a lot of those anymore. He speaks for justice, and although there's a great humility about him, there's also a pride. He knows who he is."

Whatever your perspective—had Carter emerged as a great moral leader, or was he simply a partisan scold?—it was obvious he was doing precisely what he wanted and what he thought he should. He had no intention of changing his course.

The Carter Legacy

In 2006, as this book was going to press, Jimmy Carter was approaching his eighty-second birthday. On many different fronts it was a busy time. For one thing Carter was looking for a way to reenter what was for him an old, familiar fray: the elusive pursuit of a Middle East peace.

As always he didn't shy away from controversy. In the early spring of 2006 he wrote a series of op-ed pieces, published in more than seventy newspapers, including *USA Today* and the *International Herald Tribune*. He criticized Israel for its expansionist policies in the West Bank and Gaza and argued for a viable Palestinian state as the only hope for a Middle East peace.

Carter's article of faith, supported by public-opinion polls, was that the vast majority of Israelis and Palestinians wanted a fair and stable peace and understood essentially what was necessary to achieve it. "Over the years," Carter wrote, "opinion polls have consistently shown that about 60 per cent of Israelis favor withdrawing from the West Bank in exchange for a durable peace." And in 2006, even after the militant group Hamas won control of the Palestinian parliament, more than 80 percent of Palestinians still wanted a peace agreement with Israel.

The fundamental problem, as Carter understood it, was how to fashion a political solution that matched the deepest, most decent

aspirations of the people. There had been the occasional moments of breakthrough—the Camp David Accords of 1978, arguably the high point of the Carter presidency, and the Oslo agreements of 1993, in which the United States helped broker a deal between Israel and the PLO.

Three Israelis and their Arab counterparts had received the Nobel Prize for their courage, and two of the leaders—Yitzhak Rabin and Anwar Sadat—were later murdered by Middle Eastern extremists. Despite the heroism of such men, sealed in blood, the level of hostility had continued to worsen. During a five-year period ending in March 2006 more than 3,900 Palestinians and nearly 1,100 Israelis had been killed in the escalating conflict, "and this," wrote Carter, "includes many children: 708 Palestinians and 123 Israelis."

In his writings, as well as in his conversations with world leaders, Carter tried to make the case for restraint. But over the years he was not content with merely stating his opinion. Working through the Carter Center, he had met with key Palestinian leaders, including Yasir Arafat, to urge a reconciliation with Israel. In his book *The Blood of Abraham*, a kind of Middle East primer published in 1985, Carter lamented the violence of the PLO and its stubborn refusal to recognize Israel. "By following its present policies of confrontation and inflexibility," Carter wrote, "the PLO has not gained one inch of territory or any other advantage for the Palestinians."

In 1990 Carter and Arafat finally met face-to-face, a private meeting in Paris, and Carter again urged a course of restraint, including an explicit recognition of Israel. He also revealed the depth of his sympathy for Palestinian suffering. "This is an obsession with me," he declared. Arafat seemed moved. Carter always had a gift for that. He could say simple things that came from his heart, and there were ways in which the Middle East agony could resonate powerfully in his southerner's mind.

He was raised in a time of racial division, of second-class standing for a whole group of people and the easy rationalizations of their neighbors in power, including members of his family. As with many white southerners of conscience he could identify with the oppressors, as well as the oppressed, and that provided his indignation with an edge. He understood the insidious lure of injustice.

In the coming months Carter began giving Arafat advice. "Emphasize peace, not violence," he wrote. Talk about grievances—the closing of Palestinian universities, homes destroyed by Israeli bulldozers, Palestinians imprisoned without legal counsel—but talk also about common ground. There were people in Washington willing to listen, for President George H. W. Bush and Secretary of State James Baker were reasonable men, Carter said, able to understand Palestinian concerns.

Carter continued his litany for the next several years, treating Arafat with unaccustomed respect and trying to convince him that negotiations could succeed where threats and terrorism had failed. By the early months of the Clinton administration a new optimism about the possibility of peace had emerged, as the Israelis and the PLO began direct negotiations in Norway. By September 1993 they had managed to reach an historic accord—PLO recognition of Israel in exchange for self-governance in parts of the Palestinian territory. It was a watershed moment that many observers thought would have been impossible without Jimmy Carter. Historian Douglas Brinkley called it "a monument" to Carter's tenacity. From Camp David forward, Brinkley wrote, "Carter pressed harder and more consistently for a political solution to the Arab-Israeli impasse than any other diplomat on the world stage. Even when he had no official role, he never let up. . . . Carter had been ruthless in the pursuit of peace."

His involvement didn't end with the Oslo accords. On three different occasions, beginning in 1996, Carter led international

teams to monitor Palestinian elections. The Carter Center's pattern was now well established: Working with the National Democratic Institute, a nonprofit organization created by Congress, the center sent in teams before the election to help participants agree on the rules, assure fair access to the media, and avoid political intimidation or oppression. On election day the teams, which ranged in size from forty members in 1996 to eighty-five a decade later, fanned out across the West Bank, Gaza, and East Jerusalem to observe the voting process itself.

All three elections featured at least a few moments of disagreement or contention, primarily in East Jerusalem. This was bitterly disputed land, the Palestinian section of the holy city that was now controlled by the Israelis. To emphasize its sovereignty, the Israeli government required Palestinians to vote with absentee ballots dropped into boxes at six Jerusalem post offices. In all three elections there was tension, confusion, and sporadic confrontation as thousands of East Jerusalem Palestinians came to vote but discovered problems with the registration process.

The Carter Center's David Carroll recalled the scene in 2005—a large and sullen Palestinian crowd massed outside the main post office, many of them told that they could not vote. Their names were not on the list for that particular post office. With the Palestinians growing more visibly angry, Carter set out to find a solution. He met with Israeli postal officials and called Prime Minister Ariel Sharon, and within two hours he was able to defuse a tense situation. "He worked out an agreement," Carroll explained, "under which any Palestinians who could show they had registered to vote in East Jerusalem could vote at any of the six post offices. He went in and explained this to the postal officials and then came out and shouted an explanation to the massive crowd of Palestinians. They seemed to accept it, and we knew that Carter had helped avert a serious problem."

To Carter, however, the moment was mostly unremarkable—inevitable in such a troubled part of the world. The important thing was that, in three different elections, the Palestinian people had demonstrated their pride and democratic tenacity. "It is almost a miracle," Carter said. Even in the election of 2006, when the Palestinians elected a parliament dominated by Hamas, Carter continued to see hope for peace. Hamas, after all, was a part of the Palestinian landscape, a reflection of the deep frustration of the people.

The question was how to steer the frustration toward negotiation rather than violence. In that regard the Carter Center maintained its offices in the West Bank city of Ramallah, intending among other things to monitor upcoming municipal elections. Carter's hope was that the largest Palestinian factions—Hamas and the Fatah Party of Palestinian president Mahmoud Abbas—would be able to reach some common understanding, thus providing the Israelis with a single negotiating partner for peace.

At the time the center was pursuing these objectives, Carter was expanding his op-ed pieces from early 2006 into a book called *Palestine: Peace Not Apartheid.* He argued controversially that the government of Israel had veered to the right, relying too heavily on naked force—on its military might and the building of a wall across the West Bank—to end the threat of Palestinian terrorism. Based on Israeli death tolls among other evidence, Carter thought the strategy had been a devastating failure, and he called, as he had so often in the past, for a course of negotiation and restraint. "The spilled blood in the Holy Land still cries out to God," Carter wrote, "an anguished cry for peace."

Despite the eloquence of Carter's appeal supporters of Israel were quick to take offense at his framing of the issue. The prominent Jewish lawyer Alan Dershowitz, in a searing review, accused Carter of writing "an indecent book" filled with "hyperbole and

overstatement" that demonstrated "bias against Israel." Dershowitz said Carter's use of the term "apartheid" was "especially outrageous."

Responding during an interview on *Larry King Live*, Carter refused to back away from either the tone or the substance of the book. "The oppression of Palestinians by Israeli forces . . . is horrendous," he said, "one of the worst cases of oppression I know of." Carter said he knew when he wrote it that the book was certain to be controversial. But that, he added, was precisely the point—"to precipitate some controversy . . . to promote debate," particularly within the United States, where the issue so often was simply brushed aside.

In response to the book, and Carter's defense of it, fourteen members resigned en masse from the Carter Center's advisory board, and other critics, as Carter later noted, accused him of being "a liar and a bigot and an anti-Semite and a coward." But despite the growing swirl of controversy Carter pushed ahead, accepting an invitation to speak at Brandeis University, the Jewish-sponsored institution in Massachusetts.

On January 23, 2007, addressing more than seventeen hundred Brandeis students, faculty, and staff, Carter sketched out his reverence for Jewish history—both the Old Testament stories he had grown up with and essentially memorized in his Sunday school classes and the more recent example of Louis Brandeis, for whom the university was named. Carter praised Brandeis, who in 1916 became the first Jewish member of the U.S. Supreme Court, both for his advocacy of freedom of speech and his activist support for the founding of Israel.

Carter spoke also about his presidential decision to create the United States Holocaust Memorial Museum, with a commission chaired by Elie Wiesel. "I understand completely," he continued, "the fear among many Israelis that threats still exist against their safety and even their existence as a nation. During all these

years . . . I have reiterated my strong condemnation of any acts of terrorism, which are not justified at any time or for any goal. I have spent a great deal of my adult life trying to bring peace to Israel and its neighbors, based on justice and righteousness for the Palestinians."

But at Brandeis, as he had in other places, Carter reiterated his criticism of Israeli policies toward the West Bank. Israel's settlements, he said, had taken "choice hilltops, vital water resources, and productive land," and that confiscation, along with a forty-foot security wall through much of the Palestinian territory, "makes the lives of Palestinians almost intolerable."

When the speech was over, Alan Dershowitz, who was also speaking at Brandeis that night, praised the tone that Carter had taken. But he also declared, "There are two different Jimmy Carters." And Deborah Lipstadt, professor of Jewish studies at Emory, who had written in the *Washington Post* that Carter's book makes only "fleeting references to the Holocaust," continued her criticisms after Brandeis.

Eli Evans, one of the great Jewish writers from the South, whose book *The Provincials* was a regional classic, observed the whole episode with dismay. "The book was just not like Carter," he said. "He had been such an extraordinarily fair-minded peacemaker—a president who, because of Camp David, was able to conceive the Carter Center as an effective institution of peace. But now here he was bringing the weight of a Nobel Prize to give credibility to Arab propaganda—that everything was Israel's fault." Carter, said Evans, seemed to have come to see the Middle East through a southerner's eyes, "simplifying it as a racial conflict with the same civil rights dimensions he had known in the South—overlooking the profound religious, cultural, and historical lessons that made it so dramatically different."

Evans maintained that Carter's book gave little attention to the specter of Iran—a country whose president, Mahmoud Ahmadi-

nejad, was a Holocaust denier on the verge of obtaining a nuclear weapon. With the Holocaust still a living memory the malevolent rhetoric of Iran—and its provision of weapons to anti-Israeli extremists—raised new fears of "annihilation." But Carter, in his book, had virtually ignored that ominous reality and directed his criticism at Israel. In addition, Evans said the use of the word "apartheid" in the title "is widely considered an inflammatory distortion of history," and he predicted the whole episode "could well affect Jimmy Carter's legacy."

As the controversy gained momentum through the winter, there were a few scattered voices in Carter's defense. Paul Findley, a former Republican congressman from Illinois, wrote in a column for the *Chicago Tribune* that "at the age of 82, Jimmy Carter entered the lion's den. . . . He deserves a hero's praise." And Chris Hedges, defending Carter in the *Nation*, maintained that, if anything, the former president didn't go far enough. "Carter's book exposes little about Israel," wrote Hedges, a former Middle East correspondent for the *New York Times*. "The enforced segregation, abject humiliation and spiraling Israeli violence against the Palestinians have been detailed in the Israeli and European press and, with remarkable consistency, by all the major human rights organizations. . . . The bleakness of life for Palestinians, especially in the Gaza Strip, is a mystery only to us."

It was a mystery Carter intended to dispel, and he remained convinced that he had achieved part of what he set out to do: He had forced a debate in the United States on the wisdom and justice of Israel's policies. To the extent he succeeded, it was probably true that only Carter could have done it. Not many American leaders had the nerve—or some might say, the diffident certainty of point of view—to wade headlong into those troubled waters, risking reputation in the process.

But the debate that Carter set out to provoke lay, in a sense, at the heart of his legacy—the passionate pursuit of justice and peace,

bolstered by the stubborn depth of his resolve. It was, of course, a controversial legacy, created over the course of thirty years and consisting, ultimately, of at least two parts. The first was his presidency, those four tumultuous years in the White House where the reviews, inevitably, would continue to be mixed. Historian Dan Carter, no relation to the president, summarized his tenure this way:

> Jimmy Carter's political failings were serious. He seldom sought to conceal his conviction that he was dead right and his opponents were dunces—not a useful trait when dealing with important and self-important members of Congress.
>
> At the same time, it now seems clear that there were positive aspects of the Carter presidency that have been overlooked or, at the very least, not given the weight they deserve. While he is often credited for his accomplishments in Middle Eastern diplomacy, we take for granted his success in such areas as Latin American relations. And I don't think that we've given Carter nearly enough credit for his leadership in the critical area of energy conservation.

Beyond the details of presidential policy, fodder for the next generation of historians, there was also the revealing story from Jim Laney, former president of Emory University and U.S. ambassador to South Korea. Laney had worked with the recently deposed former president to create the center that now bears his name—and he did it in partnership with Emory, one of the nation's most prestigious universities.

Not everyone was pleased with that decision, including some on Emory's board of trustees. In 1981, when the discussions for a center were first taking place, Carter was widely viewed as a failure. He had lost overwhelmingly to Ronald Reagan, and the media understanding of his time in the White House was one of a leader out of his depth. "The early days of the Carter Center were hard days," said Laney. Funding was scarce, criticism common, and Carter himself was fighting his way through his own disappoint-

ment. But then one day, Carter and Laney were walking across campus, and they met Karl Deutsch, one of the country's most distinguished political scientists, who had come to Emory after a long stay at Harvard.

Laney introduced Deutsch and Carter, who had never met, and Deutsch declared with obvious emotion that in contrast to most American politicians, Carter would still be remembered a thousand years from now—the first and only U.S. president who had made human rights the cornerstone of policy. "Carter," said Laney, "had tears in his eyes."

If Deutsch was right, and the big-picture truth about Jimmy Carter will one day obscure the bumps and failures that went with his presidency, there may in the end be even less debate about the second part of his legacy, his time out of office. Jay Hakes, director of the Carter Presidential Library, has argued plausibly that Carter has "redefined the modern postpresidency." If that is so, the journey has not been without controversy. Supporters of Israel have questioned Carter's bias, and conservative American political commentators have criticized his one-man missions for peace. But for many Americans, the dominant image that defines Carter's legacy is a former president sweating in the sun, building houses for Habitat for Humanity, or teaching his Sunday school classes in Plains, or touching the sufferers of third-world disease. He could be so tender in those situations, so completely without condescension or distance. He had said many times in many different places that the poor were a lot like everybody else—every bit as hard working or ambitious as he was, and the fundamental privilege that came with his work was to get to know such people face-to-face.

There may have been those who doubted that he meant it, but Toni Miller was not one of them. She was a single mother in Watts, and for a week in the summer of 1995, she worked side by side with President Carter on a house that she and her family would soon own. When the work was completed, Carter gave her a hug and

presented her a Bible, and Miller, who had carried herself all week with dignity and reserve, suddenly found herself unable to speak. A tear drifted softly down her cheek, and when her son reached out to brush it away, Carter, also visibly moved, reached out gently to touch her on the arm. It was, said Miller, a moment that added new meaning to her life.

For Carter, such occasions were never just photo ops, feel-good moments to share with the world. The problems were far too serious for that, and the political assumption that underlay his work was that the growing disparity between rich and poor was the number one problem facing humankind. The issue was also rooted in his faith. The Bible, as he read it, was abundant in its warnings to the rich and its admonitions about justice for the poor, and Carter was inclined to take them seriously. And finally, of course, there was the simple fact that Carter was a southerner. He had come of age in an era of injustice that gave way to the moral force of civil rights. All of those things had stamped his understanding of the world, becoming intertwined with his energy and drive and his stubborn ambition to do what was right.

As his postpresidential career unfolded, he was drawn to an expanding idea of human rights—for Carter, it was a moral force of extraordinary power that extended beyond the political realm. "During the past two decades," he wrote, not long after winning the Nobel Prize, "my concept of human rights has grown to include not only the right to live in peace, but also to adequate health care, shelter, food and economic opportunity." And despite the pain in every corner of the world, he was able to hold fast to his own leap of faith: "We can make this broad-based concept of human rights a universally accepted foundation for peace."

For Rosalynn Carter, the tangible proof of greater possibility was in the record of the past thirty years. "Jimmy's legacy," she said, "will be human rights and peace." Despite her fierce inclination to defend him, she did not argue that he had never made mistakes.

But she did believe there was probably nobody who had worked at it harder—who had made greater use of his own moral power or who had spoken the truth as he understood it with a courage and tenacity that some might even have interpreted as arrogance.

In the process he had built the Carter Center, perhaps the most tangible piece of his legacy. It was, he hoped, an institution that could stand on its own, fighting disease, monitoring elections, intervening diplomatically in the scattered civil wars that continued to ravage the global landscape. "We have reached a point," said David Carroll, "where the Carter Center name carries great weight. We have benefited from the reputation of President Carter, and we are able to do great things even without his direct involvement."

But if the center's reputation had achieved a certain independence from its founder, Carroll and others were quick to point out that there had been no decline in Carter's activity. "He is a driven man," said Carroll in the summer of 2006. "He is nearly eighty-two, but he could be here ten years from now." The assessment was widely shared among Carter's associates, for even with the first intimations of frailty—the lines on his face, the thinning gray hair and subtle stoop of his shoulders—nobody could imagine him fading away. There was too much to do. There had been sixty wars since the cold war ended, including, in 2006, the devastating firefights between Israel and the Hezbollah forces in Lebanon. There were still a few cases of guinea worm disease, still people going hungry, and there were historic elections looming just ahead.

In Carter's mind, none of that left much time for looking back, reflecting on the past or worrying about how he might be perceived. His interviews at the age of eighty-one were much like those at every stage of his career. He was obsessed with the challenges that lay just ahead—all those things still waiting to be done.

If time was shorter now than it had been, that was all the more reason to keep up the pace.

Notes and Acknowledgments

This book is a work of journalism as much as history, for the subject remains a moving target. The legacy of Jimmy Carter is still being made.

For that reason, in the course of my research, I have relied on interviews as much as any other tool, and I am grateful to the following people for their time: President Jimmy Carter, Rosalynn Carter, Dan Ariail, Robert Sam Anson, Lee Atwater, James David Barber, Will Campbell, David Carroll, Dan Carter, Hodding Carter, Eleanor Clift, Deanna Congilio, Robert Cox, Marion Creekmore, Patricia Derian, Faye Dill, Hedley Donovan, Mike Egan, Stuart Eizenstat, Eli Evans, James Fallows, Art Field, John Hope Franklin, Linda Fuller, Millard Fuller, William Greider, Jay Hakes, Tom T. Hall, Paul Hemphill, Diane Higgins, Steve Hochman, Matthew Hodes, Donald Hopkins, Ray Jenkins, Hamilton Jordan, James Laney, William Leuchtenburg, Yawei Liu, Robert Maddox, Julia Maulden, Jennifer McCoy, Toni Miller, Robert Pastor, Jody Powell, Gerald Rafshoon, Marly Rusoff, Gary Sick, Jacobo Timerman, John Turner, James Wall, Miller Williams, Pamela Willoughby, and James Young.

Some of these interviews took place in the spring and summer of 1985 when I was working on a series of articles about Carter and his presidency for the *Charlotte Observer*. Others took place in 1995 and 1996 when I was researching a book on Habitat for Humanity. And finally I did another round of interviews in the spring and summer of 2006 as I was concluding the research for this book.

I have also drawn on the work of other journalists, including two important early profiles of Carter: "Looking for Jimmy," by Robert Sam

Anson, which appeared August 6, 1976, in *New Times* magazine; and "A Carter Album," by William Greider, which appeared in the *Washington Post* on October 25, 1976. In November 1976 *Playboy* magazine published an insightful and eventually famous interview with Carter, and in the years since then I have read and benefited from numerous articles in other publications, including *Africa Today*, the *Atlanta Journal-Constitution*, the *Charlotte Observer*, the *Hartford Courant*, the *Houston Chronicle*, the *Journal of Democracy*, *National Geographic*, *Newsweek*, the *New York Times*, *Time*, and the *Washington Post*.

The literature on Carter has expanded steadily through the years, and the following books proved especially useful for the quotes, insight, and information they contain: *The Presidential Character*, by James David Barber; *The Unfinished Presidency*, by Douglas Brinkley; *Why Not the Best?, Keeping Faith, The Blood of Abraham, Always a Reckoning, An Hour before Daylight, Living Faith, Our Endangered Values*, and *Palestine: Peace Not Apartheid*, by Jimmy Carter; *A Moment of Crisis: Jimmy Carter, the Power of a Peacemaker, and North Korea's Nuclear Ambitions*, by Marion Creekmore; *From Roosevelt to Reagan*, by Hedley Donovan; *Love in the Mortar Joints*, by Millard Fuller; *Crisis: The Last Year of the Carter Presidency*, by Hamilton Jordan; *With God on Our Side*, by William Martin; *Not Doomed to Repetition*, by Robert A. Pastor; *The Spiritual Journey of Jimmy Carter*, by Wesley Pippert; *Jimmy Carter: President and Peacemaker*, by David Seidman; *All Fall Down: America's Tragic Encounter with Iran*, by Gary Sick; and *Going Critical: The First North Korean Nuclear Crisis*, by Joel S. Wit, Daniel B. Poneman, and Robert L. Gallucci.

Any serious student of President Carter, of course, must also spend time at the Carter Library and Museum in Atlanta, and I am grateful for the resources those institutions provide. Among other things the library has considerable footage from CNN, which, in part because of its base in Atlanta, has done an extensive job of covering Jimmy Carter and his activities, particularly those of his postpresidency. The Carter Center's Web site is replete with helpful and accurate material. I am also grateful to Deanna Congilio, the press secretary to President and Mrs. Carter, who went out of her way to make sure I had the information I needed.

Here, chapter by chapter, are the sources I, as well as David Carter in his elegant foreword, relied on for this account. My purpose here is to

acknowledge my debts and to explain the synthesis of my own understanding. Any flaws in perspective are entirely my own.

Foreword

The quotes from Jack Nelson, Tom T. Hall, and James Wall about my initial writings on Carter are contained in letters they wrote to me. Roger Wilkins's comments about Carter were made on PBS's program *The News Hour with Jim Lehrer* on May 17, 2002. The quote "I don't think we ought to put bronze on him yet" came from author and journalist Haynes Johnson on that same broadcast.

Vice President Dick Cheney's quote about conservation appeared in the *Washington Post* on May 1, 2001. Carter's "crisis of the American spirit" quote was taken from his speech "Energy and National Goals," the so-called malaise speech, delivered July 15, 1979. His observations about preventive war came from his Nobel Peace Prize lecture, December 10, 2002.

John Kennedy's elegant quote about peace was part of his commencement address at American University, June 10, 1963. Julian Bond's remembrance of President Lyndon Johnson is quoted in *Exploring the Johnson Years*, published by the University of Texas Press in 1981.

Prologue

I attended Jimmy Carter's speech at Wingate College on February 5, 1985, and wrote about it for the next day's *Charlotte Observer*. I don't know the identity of the young man who rose during the question-and-answer session to praise President Carter for his contributions. But his quotes, along with Carter's, are based on my notes from that occasion and appeared in the *Charlotte Observer* in February and also on July 7, 1985.

William Leuchtenburg's quote about Carter ("It was as if he were a rock star") was offered in an interview with me in February 1985. The statistics and accounts of Carter's 1985 national tour in promotion of his book *The Blood of Abraham* came from his agent, Marly Rusoff, and his publisher's representative, Diane Higgins. John Zakarian's account of another successful Carter appearance at about the same time appeared in the *Hartford Courant*. James David Barber's summary of Carter—his

failures were failures of technique, his triumphs were triumphs of character—was offered in one of a series of interviews that I did with Barber in the spring and early summer of 1985.

Douglas Brinkley's quotation from Dylan Thomas appears in Brinkley's book *The Unfinished Presidency*.

Chapter One

The descriptions of Sumter County, Georgia, and the surrounding area are based on my own observations, including my visit to the Andersonville historic site. I also visited Koinonia Farms on a number of occasions and heard the story of Clarence Jordan's face-off with the Ku Klux Klan from his close friends Millard Fuller and Will Campbell. Fuller tells Jordan's story in his book *Love in the Mortar Joints*.

Other than Carter's own book *Why Not the Best?* one of the best accounts of the defining forces of his early political career can be found in James David Barber's *The Presidential Character*. Barber tells, with extraordinary insight, the story of Carter's defiance of the White Citizens' Council. The characterization of Carter as a kind of real-life Atticus Finch in regard to race—not a crusader, but a man who didn't hide his sympathies—is mine but is corroborated by Barber's understandings and also by interviews with Carter and his wife Rosalynn in 1985. Rosalynn Carter's memory of "real arguments" between Jimmy Carter and his father was offered in her interview with me.

Jody Powell, Hamilton Jordan, and Gerald Rafshoon, in their interviews with me, all described Carter's participation in the 1972 Democratic National Convention and their failed ambition to have him nominated for vice president. It was Rafshoon who remembered the quote "Governor, we'd like to have a talk about your future," which referred to his young aides' hopes that he would run for president.

In our series of interviews in 1985 Carter told me he had warned his associates after the 1972 convention not to tell anybody about his presidential ambitions because "it sounds too ridiculous." Rosalynn Carter has made the point many times about her husband's self-confidence and his ability to believe he could accomplish whatever he set out to do. One

of those occasions was during her 1985 interview with me, and the observation appeared in the *Charlotte Observer* on July 7, 1985.

Carter's quote "We memorized all of the state election laws" was offered in a 1985 conversation we had in Plains and also appeared in the *Charlotte Observer* on July 7, 1985. Many people have testified about the startling force of Carter's intelligence in one-to-one or small group sessions. James David Barber wrote about it, Patricia Derian talked to me about it, and I had the same experience on my own. James Fallows, the widely respected Washington editor for the *Atlantic Monthly*, offered his assessment of that particular Carter skill in a 1985 interview with me. His quotes appeared in the *Observer* on July 7.

Carter's eloquent quote about "the moral and ethical standards of our nation" was not a prepared sound bite but rather a spontaneous observation during our interview in Plains. Patricia Derian remembered similar affirmations from her own early conversations with Carter and remembered how deeply she had been impressed.

Eleanor Clift of *Newsweek* offered her mistaken assessment that Carter was "FDR and Harry Truman rolled into one" in a 1985 conversation with me. The quote, along with others in this chapter, also appeared in the *Charlotte Observer* in July 1985.

Journalist Robert Sam Anson wrote with both astonishment and insight about Carter's religious faith in his superb *New Times* profile "Looking for Jimmy," published August 6, 1976. Anson and I also talked in 1985 about how easy it was to be impressed by Carter's aura of good will and intelligence. The quotes from Robert Maddox about Carter's faith and from Hamilton Jordan about the complexity of Carter's character appeared in the July 7, 1985, *Charlotte Observer* and were based on interviews with me.

Chapter Two

I had the honor of interviewing Jacobo Timerman for the *Charlotte Observer* series on Carter, and his quotes appeared on July 8, 1985. Patricia Derian and Robert Cox also talked with me at length about Carter's human rights policies, and Derian described in some detail how she

negotiated improvements with some of the world's most notorious human rights violators.

I had the good fortune of talking about the subtleties of Carter's faith with his fellow—and equally devout—Southern Baptists Robert Maddox and Will Campbell, and with James Wall, editor of the *Christian Century* magazine. I also drew on Wesley Pippert's fine book *The Spiritual Journey of Jimmy Carter* and on Carter's interview with *Playboy* magazine published in November 1976. Later I read Carter's own book *Living Faith*.

Carter's quote about nuclear retaliation ("I would not hesitate") is based on Robert Maddox's recounting of what was for him an unforgettable congressional briefing. The quote appeared in the *Charlotte Observer* on July 8, 1985.

The account of the Camp David negotiations is based on conversations I had with Carter and his press secretary Jody Powell and on Carter's detailed account in his presidential memoir *Keeping Faith*. My own synthesis of that historic event, including Powell's quote about Carter aiming high, appeared in the *Charlotte Observer* on July 8, 1985. Carter's facetious suggestion to Israeli prime minister Menachem Begin that he simply sign Egypt's initial negotiating proposal "as written" in order to "save us all a lot of time" is taken from Carter's account in *Keeping Faith*, as is Begin's reply.

Carter's quote about his acrimonious exchange with Begin ("I stood up for Begin to leave") also appears in *Keeping Faith*. William Leuchtenburg's reflections on Carter's leadership—his inability to offer hope for the people of his own country—were offered in an interview with me and published in the *Charlotte Observer* on July 8, 1985.

Chapter Three

In an interview with me, Ray Jenkins, a fine southern journalist and former Carter assistant, recalled his conversation with UN Secretary General Kurt Waldheim about Waldheim's encounter with an Iranian mob. The anecdote appeared in the July 9, 1985, *Charlotte Observer*. So did the observation from Democratic leader Robert Strauss that Carter had used up all his luck getting elected president and had none left for his last year

of office. The *Atlantic Monthly*'s James Fallows relayed that observation to me in an interview during the spring of 1985.

William Greider wrote about Carter's 1962 campaign for the Georgia Senate in the *Washington Post* on October 25, 1976, and James David Barber relied in part on Greider's account in his book *The Presidential Character*. In my own recounting of the 1962 election I relied on both Barber and Greider. The quote from Carter's friend John Pope about how winning suddenly "meant everything" to Carter appears in *The Presidential Character*.

Hamilton Jordan told me the story of Carter's abrupt behavior after losing the 1966 governor's race in Georgia. The anecdote appeared in the July 9, 1985, *Charlotte Observer*. Mike Egan, a Republican ally of Carter's during his term as governor, offered his thoughtful assessment of Carter's political style in an interview with me, also quoted in the *Charlotte Observer*, July 9.

Former House Speaker Tip O'Neill wrote about Jimmy Carter's lack of understanding of Washington politics in his autobiography, *Man of the House: The Life and Political Memoirs of Speaker Tip O'Neill*. Douglas Brinkley also quoted O'Neill in *The Unfinished Presidency*. Jim Young of the University of Virginia, coordinator of an ambitious oral history project on Carter, talked with me about how Carter's pristine view of public service often got in his way. Young's views appeared in the July 9, 1985, *Charlotte Observer*.

William Greider's quote "Jimmy Carter as a person is so immensely confident of his virtue" was offered in an interview with me and appeared in the same issue of the *Charlotte Observer*. The same was true of Jody Powell's account of Carter dropping out of a long-distance run in the hills of Maryland. Gerry Rafshoon recalled for me Carter's inept insistence on quoting his daughter Amy in the 1980 presidential debates, and Rafshoon's observation "It's so bad that it's funny" appeared in the July 9, 1985, *Charlotte Observer*. So did Hedley Donovan's comparison of the leadership styles of Carter and Reagan.

The quote from Carter pollster Pat Caddell "It's going to be a big Reagan victory" appears in Hamilton Jordan's book *Crisis: The Last Year of the*

Carter Presidency. My characterization of Caddell as "abrasive" is based, in part, on his reputation and on my own brief encounter with him.

Chapter Four

My synthesis of the hostage crisis in Iran is based in part on daily newspaper accounts from those troubled days but primarily on three overview accounts: Hamilton Jordan's recollections in his book *Crisis*; Jimmy Carter's in his memoir *Keeping Faith*; and national security adviser Gary Sick's in his book *All Fall Down: America's Tragic Encounter with Iran*. In addition, I interviewed Jordan, Carter, and Sick, as well as Eleanor Clift, *Newsweek's* White House correspondent during that difficult year. My first attempt to write the Iranian hostage story, including each of the quotes in this chapter, appeared in the *Charlotte Observer* on July 10, 1985.

Carter, Sick, and Jordan all wrote about Jordan's cloak-and-dagger negotiations with Iranian foreign minister Sadegh Ghotbzadeh. Most of the details, including the quotes from Ghotbzadeh, are taken from Jordan's book, because he was the person most clearly in the position to know what happened in his one-on-one talks with the Iranian. I confirmed most of those details in an interview with Jordan in 1985.

Sick offers both the clearest and most extended account of the ill-fated Iranian rescue mission in *All Fall Down*. Sick's quote "Carter's tough private message served its purpose" came from an interview with me and appeared in the *Charlotte Observer* on July 10, 1985. Carter's quote "Khomeini knew I meant it" appeared in that same issue of the *Observer* and came from my 1985 interview with Carter in Plains.

James Fallows's quote about Carter being "very good about figuring out the right thing to do" appeared in the same story. Fallows went on to say that Carter was less adept at selling his decisions in the political marketplace. Gary Sick's parallel observation about Carter's belief that the right decision "would sell itself" appeared first in *All Fall Down* and was quoted again in the July 10, 1985, *Charlotte Observer*. Carter's lengthy reflections on the Iranian crisis appeared in that same issue of the *Observer*, and the quotes were taken from our interview in Plains.

James David Barber, a scholar of extraordinary generosity, made time

for numerous conversations while I was working on the Carter series, and his astute observation about our national mythology regarding the presidency came from those conversations.

Chapter Five

The Reverend Dan Ariail's quote "he's just Jimmy" appeared in the July 11, 1985, *Charlotte Observer*, as did Ray Jenkins's eloquent quote "Bitterness is the black beast that stalks politicians." The quotes from Carter in his Sunday school class appeared in that same issue and were based on a class that I attended in the early summer of 1985.

In 1995–96 I spent nearly two years working on a book titled *If I Were a Carpenter: Twenty Years of Habitat for Humanity*, and in the course of that project I interviewed Habitat founder Millard Fuller multiple times about his organization's history and Jimmy Carter's unique role. I also interviewed Carter in 1995 during a house-building project in the Los Angeles neighborhood of Watts. My synthesis of the Habitat story for this book is based on those interviews, as well as Fuller's account in his book *Love in the Mortar Joints*. The quotes from Fuller's spiritual mentor, Clarence Jordan, are taken from Fuller's book.

I covered Jimmy Carter's talk about Habitat for Humanity in Charlotte, North Carolina, and the quotes appear in *If I Were a Carpenter*. Carter's quote "It's not a bad life," from 1985, as well as his extended reflections on his presidency, on Ronald Reagan, and on his future, were based on our interview in Plains and appeared in the July 11, 1985, *Charlotte Observer*. So did Rosalynn Carter's fatalistic observation "We assume the record will be there for people to see . . . someday." Carter's quote about allowing Ronald Reagan to become president being "by far my biggest failure in office" appears in Douglas Brinkley's *The Unfinished Presidency*.

The assessments of Carter's presidency by Stuart Eizenstat, John Hope Franklin, Lee Atwater, and Hodding Carter appeared in the July 11, 1985, *Charlotte Observer*, as did James David Barber's summary observations. Jay Hakes's quote about Carter's environmental record was offered in an interview with me on June 14, 2006.

Chapter Six

William Safire has written numerous columns ridiculing Carter's motives and policies. The particular column about Carter's "lust in his heart" for the Nobel Prize appeared in the September 22, 1994, *New York Times*. Carter's quote "What if the Nobel were the be-all and end-all of my existence?" came in an interview with ABC's James Wooten and appears in Douglas Brinkley's *The Unfinished Presidency*.

Steve Hochman's recollections of working with Jimmy Carter on the memoir *Keeping Faith* were offered in an interview with me on May 18, 2006. The sense of Carter's restlessness in the early days of the Carter Center came from that same interview with Hochman and was confirmed in my interview with Carter on June 14, 2006. In one of the earliest in a series of conversations in the spring and summer of 2006 Deanna Congilio offered her thoughts about a breakthrough moment for the Carter Center occurring in 1989 when Carter was asked to monitor elections in Panama. The center's Jennifer McCoy had the same sense of that assignment's importance.

The account of Carter's Panama experience is based on interviews with Robert Pastor, who was, for years, Carter's top advisor on Latin America, and on the account in Douglas Brinkley's *The Unfinished Presidency*. Carter's quote "I hope there will be a worldwide outcry" is taken from Brinkley's book. Pastor's quote about Carter's "most impressive" performance was offered in an interview with me on June 2, 2006, as was his anecdote about Noriega's chief of intelligence warning, "You guys better get your asses out of here." (Pastor tells the same story in *The Unfinished Presidency*, where there is an incidental variation in the quote.)

In interviews with me in 2006 Pastor (June 21) and Jennifer McCoy (May 18) talked at length about Carter's 1990 election-monitoring trip to Nicaragua. I also relied on Pastor's book *Not Condemned to Repetition* and on his article "The Making of a Free Election," which appeared in the *Journal of Democracy* in the summer of 1990. Carter's quote about Sandinista leader Daniel Ortega, "I had to sit and listen to his rhetoric," came from an interview with me on June 14, 2006.

Carter's reassurance to the Nicaraguan people, "be confident your vote will count," is quoted in Pastor's *Not Condemned to Repetition*, as is

Carter's historic conversation with Daniel Ortega urging him to accept his defeat in the election for the long-term good of his country.

The story of Carter's encounter with rioters on election day in Guyana was told to me by Pastor and Jennifer McCoy and is recounted also in the Carter Center's Special Report 3, *Observing Guyana's Electoral Process, 1990–92*. Carter's quote "If there are riots at the election commission, we are going there" is based on the recollections of Robert Pastor. Carter's quote "I investigated, as best I could, their allegations" is taken from the transcript of a press conference Carter gave in Georgetown, Guyana, on October 6, 1992.

Deanna Congilio's assessment of the Carter Center's progress in building democracy, "It's two steps forward and one step back," was offered in a conversation with me on June 14, 2006. I interviewed the Center's Yawei Liu on June 26, 2006, and David Carroll on June 14, 2006. Their quotes came from those interviews.

Chapter Seven

Carter talked about the evolution of the Carter Center in our June 14, 2006, interview. Also on June 14 David Carroll offered his observation about Carter's extraordinary ability to focus. The story of the Carters' first personal encounter with guinea worm disease was related to me by President Carter and by the Carter Center's Donald Hopkins, who was there and who confirmed and expanded on the details of Carter's telling. The anecdote also appeared in shorter form in the March 26, 2006, *New York Times*. It was part of an extraordinary *Times* series on third-world diseases, including guinea worm and lymphatic filariasis. In November 2005 *National Geographic* also published material on the Carter Center's campaign against guinea worm, and on October 9, 2005, the *Houston Chronicle* did an in-depth report on river blindness. The publication *Africa Today* covered some of the same ground in September 2005.

Carter and Hopkins told me about former UN official Peter Bourne's important role in making Carter aware of the guinea worm problem. In addition, Douglas Brinkley wrote about Bourne in *The Unfinished Presidency*. The statistics on guinea worm and other diseases came primarily from Hopkins, who coordinates the Carter Center's health-care efforts.

Carter's quote about the last remaining cases of guinea worm came from his interview with me. So did Hopkins's quote about the deep satisfaction of the work.

My account of Carter's peace mission to North Korea is based on interviews in the summer of 2006 with Marion Creekmore, who accompanied Carter on the mission; Rosalynn Carter, who was also there; and James Laney, former president of Emory University, who was ambassador to South Korea when Carter made the trip. Laney, in fact, was instrumental in persuading Carter to go, fearful, as they both were, that war was looming on the Korean peninsula.

I also read the accounts of the Korean crisis in *The Unfinished Presidency* and in the quite comprehensive *Going Critical: The First North Korean Nuclear Crisis*. The latter book was written by three Clinton administration officials deeply involved in the events: Joel S. Wit, Daniel B. Poneman, and Robert L. Gallucci. Since our interview Creekmore has completed his own excellent book on the subject, *A Moment of Crisis: Jimmy Carter, the Power of a Peacemaker, and North Korea's Nuclear Ambitions*.

David Carroll's quote about the esteem in which Carter is held overseas was offered in his June 2006 interview with me, as were Creekmore's comments on the North Korean countryside ("It was very pretty") and the toughness of North Korea's first negotiator, Kim Yong Nam. In an interview on June 30, 2006, Rosalynn Carter recalled the river cruise that she and her husband took on North Korean leader Kim Il Sung's yacht. Carter's misstatement of the United States' negotiating position, offered to Kim Il Sung and broadcast on CNN, is analyzed at length in *The Unfinished Presidency* and *Going Critical*. I also discussed it with Creekmore and Laney.

Charles Krauthammer's comparison of Carter to Neville Chamberlain, quoted in *The Unfinished Presidency*, appeared in the *Washington Post* on June 24, 1994. The word "coddle," describing Carter's approach to Kim Il Sung (among other unpopular foreign leaders), was used in several places, including the title of Steven F. Hayward's book *The Real Jimmy Carter: How America's Worst Ex-president Undermines American Foreign Policy, Coddles Dictators, and Created the Party of Clinton and Kerry*.

Clinton's quote about Carter's mission, "I was glad he went," appears

in *The Unfinished Presidency*. The assessments of the trip by James Laney and Marion Creekmore, perhaps the two people closest to it other than Carter, were offered in interviews with me. As Laney noted, Carter succeeded in pulling the world from the precipice of war and laid the foundation for shutting down North Korea's nuclear program. During the eight-year period following Carter's trip, that unpredictable nation produced no plutonium, which is the easiest path to building a nuclear weapon. North Korea did, apparently, start experimenting with uranium enrichment but according to Laney and other experts was "years away" from building a bomb with that technology. The equation changed with U.S. policy under President George W. Bush, and North Korea resumed producing plutonium and, in 2006, actually tested a nuclear weapon.

The brief account of Carter's peace mission to Haiti is synthesized from interviews with Robert Pastor and Douglas Brinkley's account in *The Unfinished Presidency*, still the volume of record on Carter's postpresidency. Pastor's quote "Carter hardly flinched" came from an interview with me. So did Rosalynn Carter's fatalistic prediction about the Nobel Prize: "We decided it was never going to happen."

Chapter Eight

Nigerian Nobel laureate Wole Soyinka's denunciation of Carter's "harmful naiveté" is quoted in *The Unfinished Presidency*. The account of Carter's Cuba trip is based primarily on interviews with Jennifer McCoy, Deanna Congilio, and Rosalynn Carter. The quotes from McCoy and Mrs. Carter came from those interviews.

Also in their interviews with me Mrs. Carter and Deanna Congilio described the morning of October 10, 2002, the day President Carter's Nobel Prize was announced. The handwritten letters of congratulation from Elie Wiesel and former President George H. W. Bush, both dated October 11, 2002, are on file at the Carter Center. The Nobel committee's citation is contained in the book *The Nobel Peace Prize Lecture*, published by Simon and Schuster, which also contains Carter's Nobel address. The quotes from his talk are taken from that book.

Mrs. Carter's quote about the Carter Center's work fighting disease, "It does something to your heart," came from her June 30, 2006, interview

with me. The great Arkansas poet Miller Williams talked with me on June 12, 2006, about Jimmy Carter's determination to become a passable poet.

The synopsis of Carter's book *Our Endangered Values* is, of course, my own, an understanding supplemented by conversations with Will Campbell, Robert Maddox, James Wall, Millard Fuller, my University of South Alabama colleague John Turner, and Carter himself. I also attended Carter's Sunday school class at Maranatha Baptist Church in Plains twice and read historian William Martin's chapters on Carter in his book *With God on Our Side*. Evangelist Jim Bakker's favorable assessment of Carter appeared in the January 28, 1980, *New York Times*. Shortly after the 1980 presidential election both Bakker and one of his closest associates told me that Bakker had voted for Carter, in contrast to many of his more conservative evangelical colleagues. Robert Maddox's quote about Carter's "tactical mistake" in not fully courting the evangelical vote appears in Maddox's book *Preacher at the White House*.

Carter's quote about the marriage of fundamentalist Christianity and the right wing of the Republican Party is taken from *Our Endangered Values*. My thoughts on Carter choosing not to remain above the fray, as many elder statesmen have done in the past, were shaped in part by conversations with my University of South Alabama colleague and fellow historian Robert Houston. Will Campbell's assessment of Carter as a prophet was offered in an interview with me on July 11, 2006.

Chapter Nine

Carter's op-ed pieces from 2006 criticizing Israeli policies appeared in *USA Today*, the *International Herald Tribune*, and other publications. His quote on the deaths of children in the Middle East conflict came from Carter's March 13, 2006, article published in *Ha'aretz* and seventy other newspapers worldwide. His critical quote about PLO confrontation and violence appears in his book *The Blood of Abraham*. His quote about his sympathy for Palestinian suffering appears in Brinkley's *The Unfinished Presidency*, as do the accounts of his advice to Yasir Arafat—"Emphasize peace, not violence"—and Brinkley's summation of Carter's tenacity.

My account of the monitoring of three Palestinian elections is informed by the Carter Center reports. David Carroll's story about Carter

negotiating an agreement on Palestinian voting in East Jerusalem was related to me in our June 14, 2006, interview. The Carter Center's Steve Hochman talked to me about the writing of Carter's latest book, *Palestine: Peace Not Apartheid*, released in the fall of 2006. The quotes from the book are taken from the published version.

Alan Dershowitz's review, labeling the book "indecent," appeared in the *Huffington Post*, November 28, 2006. Carter's interview on CNN's Larry King Live aired on November 27. His exchange with Dershowitz, a man widely known for his passionate views, and some would even say his shrillness, was only one piece of the controversy that the book generated. Even Kenneth Stein, a former staff member at the Carter Center who was once Carter's top Middle East adviser, offered his own stinging rebuke.

In severing all connection with the Carter Center, Stein declared: "President Carter's book on the Middle East, a title too inflammatory to even print, is not based on unvarnished analyses; it is replete with factual errors, copied materials not cited, superficialities, glaring omissions, and simply invented segments. Aside from the one-sided nature of the book, meant to provoke, there are recollections cited from meetings where I was the third person in the room, and my notes of those meetings show little similarity to points claimed in the book. Being a former President does not give one a unique privilege to invent information."

The quotes from Carter's conciliatory speech at Brandeis came from a text posted on the university's Web site. So did Dershowitz's quote "There are two different Jimmy Carters." Deborah Lipstadt's quote in the *Washington Post* appeared on January 20, 2007. In February she continued her criticisms in correspondence with me. The quotes and observations from Eli Evans came from conversations he and I had on February 6, 13, and 18, 2007. There were non-Jewish critics of Carter as well. Even before his book was released, Nancy Pelosi, Speaker of the U.S. House of Representatives, said Carter's views did not represent those of the Democratic Party. Paul Findley's defense of Carter in the *Chicago Tribune* appeared on February 7, 2007. Chris Hedges's article in the *Nation*, also supporting Carter's views, appeared in the January 8, 2007, issue.

Historian Dan Carter's assessment of Carter came in a July 2006 inter-

view with me, as did James Laney's story about Carter's encounter with the great political scientist Karl Deutsch. I interviewed Jay Hakes, director of the Carter Presidential Library on June 14, 2006, and among other things he offered his assessment of Carter redefining the modern postpresidency.

Carter's quote about his expanding definition of human rights is taken from the Carter Center's 2002–3 annual report. Rosalynn Carter's observation "Jimmy's legacy will be human rights and peace" was offered in her June 30, 2006, interview with me. David Carroll's quote about Carter's continuing vigor also came from our June 2006 conversation. Carter's encounter with Habitat homeowner Toni Miller was an event that I witnessed in 1995.

My thanks to all of those listed above for their contributions to our understanding of Jimmy Carter and to the sense of perspective about his legacy. Thanks also to David Carter for reading and responding to my part of the manuscript, and to my wife Nancy Gaillard, who did the same. And special thanks to Amy Rogers, founding editor of the award-winning Novello Festival Press in Charlotte, North Carolina, for offering her hard, but compassionate, editor's eye as I was completing the final stages of this project. I am grateful to all.

Index

United States Holocaust Memorial
 Museum, 98
University of Georgia, 82
University of North Carolina, 2,
 23
University of South Alabama, 91
University of Virginia, 29, 57
U.S. Army Eighty-second
 Airborne Division, 80
U.S. Department of Justice, 28
U.S. House of Representatives,
 119
U.S. Secret Service, 47
U.S. State Department, 53
U.S. Supreme Court, 98
USA Today, 93–100
USS Nimitz, 39

Vance, Cyrus, 30
Vatican, the, 36
Videla, Jorge Rafaél, 15
Vietnam War, 3, 12, 23, 32, 58
Villalon, Hector, 37

Waldheim, Kurt, 24, 37
Wall, James, ix, 13

Wallace, George, 12
Washington, D.C., 26, 28–29
Washington Post, 26, 30, 78, 99
Watergate scandal, 3, 9, 11, 32, 58
Watts, Los Angeles, 59
Weizman, Ezer, 21
West Bank, 93, 96, 97
West Germany, 44
White Citizens' Council, 6–7
White House, 29
Why Not the Best? (J. Carter), 26
Wiesbaden, Germany, 47
Wiesel, Elie, 86, 98
Wilkins, Roger, x
Williams, Miller, 88
Wingate College, 1
With God on Our Side (Martin), 90
Wooten, James, 81
World Heath Organization, 83
World Trade Center, 34
World War II, 22

Yongbyon, North Korea, 73, 76
Young, Jim, 29
Youngstown, Ohio, 23

Zakarian, John, 2